501

Things <u>YOU</u>
Should Have
Learned
About...

HISTORY

METRO BOOKS
New York

An Imprint of Sterling Publishing
387 Park Avenue South
New York, NY 10016

METRO BOOKS and the distinctive Metro Books logo
are trademarks of Sterling Publishing Co., Inc.

WRITTEN BY: Alison Rattle and Alex Woolf
DESIGNER: Clare Barber
EDITOR: Catherine Knight
PUBLISHER: James Tavendale

ISBN 978-1-4351-4079-0

For information about custom editions, special
sales, and premium and corporate purchases,
please contact Sterling Special Sales at 800-805-5489
or specialsales@sterlingpublishing.com

Manufactured in China

10 9 8 7 6 5 4 3 2

www.sterlingpublishing.com

IMAGES courtesy of www.shutterstock.com;
www.istockphoto.com and www.clipart.com.

501
Things <u>YOU</u> Should Have Learned About...

HISTORY

METRO BOOKS
New York

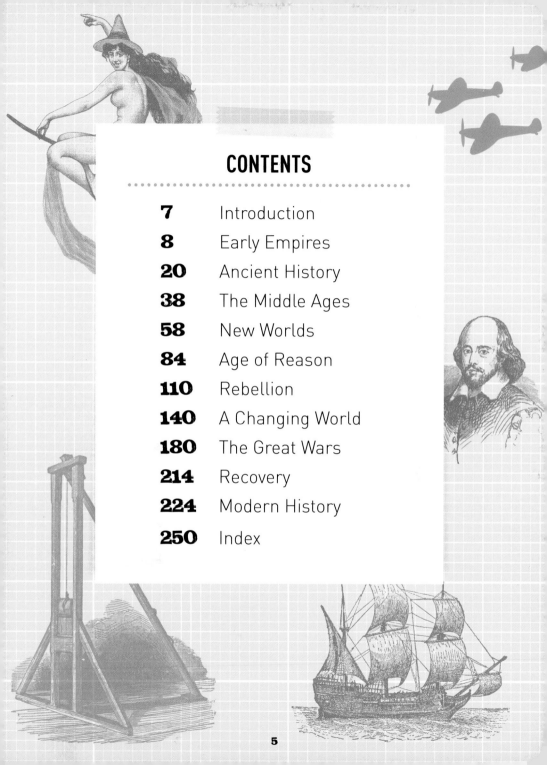

CONTENTS

INTRODUCTION

If your school days seem like ancient history and you're having trouble remembering all those dates, names and important events, this is the book for you. Beginning with the earliest civilizations, you'll follow the course of global history right up to the present day to bring your historical knowledge up to date.

Each of the 501 facts included in this book has in some way shaped the world today. Some facts are shocking, some inspiring, some are downright bizarre, but all are fascinating and have had an impact on how we live and how we think about the world around us.

History is the story of epic adventures, amazing individuals, bloody wars, ingenious inventions, daring exploits and new discoveries. This book will introduce you to the rulers of the ancient world, who had to combat political infighting and civil unrest to keep hold of their vast empires. You will sail across oceans to discover new lands with explorers such as Columbus and James Cook, learning about the founding of colonies and the first settlers. You'll experience revolutions and civil wars as groups of people fight for their right to freedom, and understand how the events of recent history have been influenced by previous centuries.

By the end of this book, you'll have a comprehensive overview of the most important events in history and be able to remember the details rather than just the names! Need to know more about the Watergate scandal, Custer's Last Stand or the Treaty of Versailles? Read on...

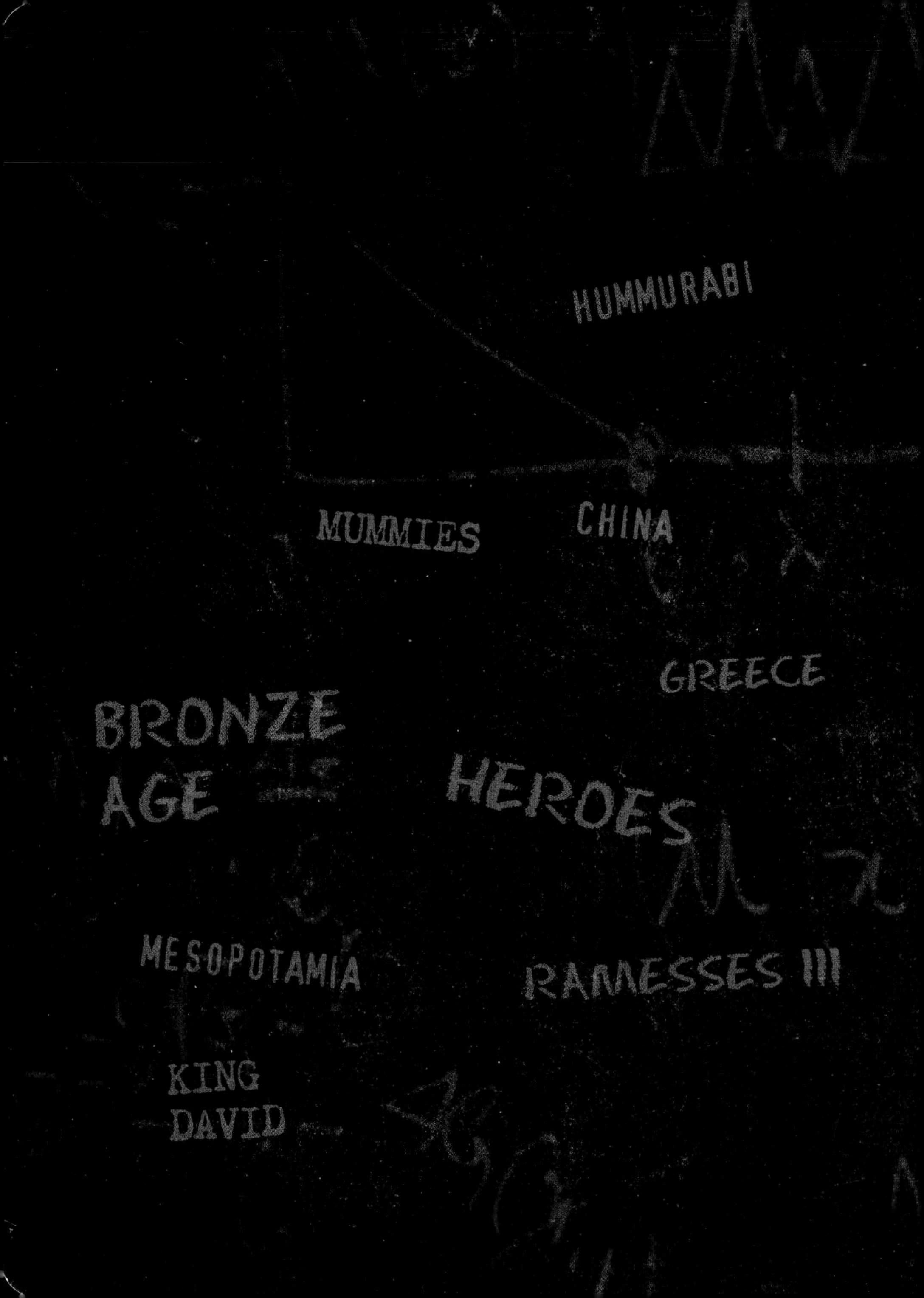

HUMMURABI

MUMMIES

CHINA

GREECE

BRONZE
AGE

HEROES

MESOPOTAMIA

RAMESSES III

KING
DAVID

MOUNT
GILBOA

KADESH

→ Early
Empires

BABYLON

EGYPT

PYRAMIDS

WHO?

PHAROHS

WHAT?

1 2900 BC THE GREAT PYRAMID IS BUILT

THE GREAT PYRAMID OF GIZA, also known as the Pyramid of Khufu or Cheops (his Greek name), is located on the Giza Plateau on the west bank of the Nile, some 12 miles southwest of Cairo. Until recently, it was the tallest man-made stone structure on earth. It is a work of mystery, incorporating exceptional engineering skills and advanced knowledge of geometry, astronomy and geodesy. It is aligned with north, south, east and west more accurately than any other known structure.

Radiocarbon dating carried out in the 1980's suggests that the pyramid was built around 2085–3809 BC, but the debate over the precise date is still ongoing. It is generally accepted that the Great Pyramid was constructed during the fourth dynasty as a tomb for the pharaoh Khufu. Archaeologists believe the architect to have been Hemiunu or Haman. As Master of Works he would have been the highest official to serve the pharaoh. Historians believe that it took a hundred thousand people over 20 years to build the pyramid, working during the three months of the Nile's annual flood.

2 FAST FACT...

ANCIENT EGYPTIAN priests removed all hair from their bodies, including their eyebrows and eyelashes.

3 FAST FACT...

AN ANCIENT EGYPTIAN CURE for blindness was mashed eyeball of pig mixed with honey and red ochre, poured into the ear.

4 FAST FACT...

MUMMIES were entombed with their mouths open so that people could eat in the afterlife.

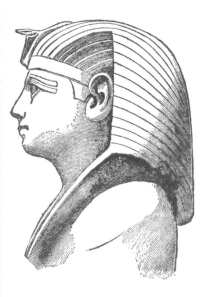

5 FAST FACT...

📖 **THE GREAT PYRAMID** is the oldest of the Seven Wonders of the Ancient World and the only one still surviving.

6 FAST FACT...

📖 **BEFORE A BODY** was mummified, the brain was pulled out through the nose.

7 2700 BC EARLY MINOAN CULTURE BEGINS

THE MINOAN CULTURE began during the Greek Bronze Age and was the first advanced civilization in Europe. In the early twentieth century, British archaeologist Sir Arthur Evans discovered and excavated the site of the palace of Knossos on the island of Crete. He named the civilization that had built it the Minoans in honor of the mythological Greek King Minos. Based on differing styles of pottery uncovered, the Minoan Period was divided into three main eras: Early Minoan, Middle Minoan and Late Minoan.

The Minoans excelled in design, the arts and producing ceramics and, thanks to their advanced maritime capabilities, their products were exported throughout the Mediterranean. They were skilled engineers and used underground clay pipes for water supply and sanitation. They were also literate, and their syllabic script, known as Linear A, has yet to be fully deciphered.

Historians believe that a natural disaster (possibly the eruption of Thera and a tsunami) caused the Minoan civilization to be wiped out around 1500 BC. This theory may also account for Plato's legend of Atlantis.

8 FAST FACT...

THE FIRST DRUNK-DRIVING conviction occurred in about 2080 BC. An Egyptian charioteer was arrested after running over a princess.

9 FAST FACT...

MESOPOTAMIAN RULER Ur-Nammu died in battle in about 2050 BC when his chariot got stuck in the mud and he fell off it.

We have been brewing tea leaves for nearly 4000 years!

10 FAST FACT...

TEA was discovered in 2373 BC by Emperor Shennong of China.

11 1900 BC THE HEROIC AGE

THE HEROIC (OR MYCENAEAN) AGE was the last chapter of the Bronze Age in Ancient Greek history. It is the historical period associated with Greek mythology and the writings of Homer.

12 FAST FACT...

OUR DIVISION of minutes and hours into units of 60 was first devised by the Sumerians of Mesopotamia (modern Iraq) in the third millennium BC.

The Mycenaeans (named after the archaeological site of Mycena in southern Greece) arrived from the north to take control of mainland Greece in around 1900 BC. They were a civilization of warriors, skilled horsemen and charioteers as well as accomplished sailors. They travelled the Aegean in their search for copper and tin to manufacture bronze and traded with Egypt and Italy. Archeologists have discovered examples of their merchandise all around the Mediterranean and as far afield as Britain. Mycenaean architecture was based on fortified cities, including Argos, Sparta, Athens and Thebes. They absorbed the skills and sophistication of the Minoans, equipping their palace bathrooms with plumbing and decorating their buildings with elaborate frescoes of heroic feats.

The Mycenaean army's greatest victory was conquering the city of Troy in around 1200 BC. Two generations later, however, the Mycenaeans were driven out of mainland Greece by a new tribe (the Dorians), whose iron weapons proved far superior to the Mycenaeans' primitive stone versions.

13 FAST FACT...

THE FIRST KNOWN CONTRACEPTIVE was crocodile dung, used by the Egyptians in about 2000 BC.

14 1780 BC THE CODE OF HAMMURABI

THE CODE OF HAMMURABI

is one of the oldest, and certainly one of the best-preserved, written legal codes in the world. Composed by the Babylonian king Hammurabi in about 1780 BC, a near-complete example of the Code, engraved on a diorite stele, was unearthed by archeologists in the ancient city of Susa (modern Iran) in 1901.

15 FAST FACT...

PUNISHMENTS in Hammurabi's 1780 law code included cutting off a man's lower lip for kissing a married woman.

King Hammurabi ruled the Amorite Dynasty of Old Babylon from around 1762–1708 BC. He was a military leader and the first Mesopotamian king to unite the various states of Mesopotamia into what would become Babylonia. In order to control and rule his vast empire of diverse peoples, he devised a set of 282 laws. These laws, or codes, covered every aspect of life from religion and slavery to marriage, military service and irrigation.

The Code is divided into three sections: the Prologue tells of the intent of the Code; the Laws lists all the actual laws; the Epilogue sets out the punishments for those who break the laws. Many modern ideas of justice and government originate from the Code, as does the famous adage "an eye for an eye and a tooth for a tooth."

16 FAST FACT...

THE OLMECS OF MEXICO began growing cocoa beans and making chocolate in around 1500 BC.

17 1274 BC THE BATTLE OF KADESH

🎓 **THE BATTLE OF KADESH** is the earliest-known recorded battle in history, and was possibly the largest chariot battle ever fought.

Egyptian forces, led by the warrior pharaoh Ramesses II, advanced on the Hittite-held city of Kadesh (on the Orontes River in Syria), in order to restore it to Egyptian rule.

The pharaoh sent four divisions of his army (one being the army of Amun led by Ramesses II himself) to approach the city from the south. Having been duped by Hittite spies into believing that the enemy army (under King Muwatallis) was much further north, Ramesses hurried towards Kadesh, hoping to surprise Muwatallis. In doing so, he unwittingly led his charioteers into a Hittite trap.

18 FAST FACT...

📖 **BY THE TIME** Ramesses II died in 1225 BC, he had fathered 96 sons and 60 daughters.

The Hittite army, which had been hiding out behind the city mound, stormed the Egyptian camp and a great battle ensued, involving over 5000 chariots.

The Gate of the Temple of Luxor

Although the two sides eventually called a truce, the battle was hailed as a great Egyptian victory and was commemorated by Ramesses II in the form of the "Poem" and the "Bulletin", and inscribed on numerous temple reliefs at Karnak, Abu Simbel, Ramesseum, Abydos and at the Temple of Luxor.

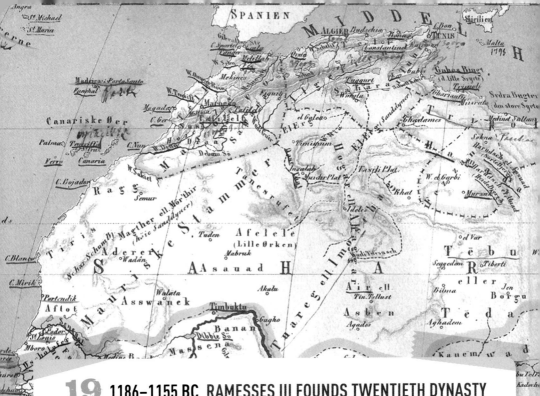

19 1186–1155 BC RAMESSES III FOUNDS TWENTIETH DYNASTY

RAMESSES III was the last of the Great Pharaohs, succeeding and continuing the work of his father, Sethnakhte, who had ruled Egypt for only two years.

By the time Ramesses III came to power, Middle East stability was on the wane and Egypt was facing its biggest threat from tribes of invaders, known as the Sea Peoples, from the Syrian and Aegean coast. When the attack finally came during his eighth year as pharaoh, Ramesses was well prepared, having secured the mouth of the Nile with his fleet of ships and installed a defensive line in Southern Palestine. The Sea Peoples were defeated and the remainder of Ramesses's 31-year reign passed in relative peace. His achievements, including the many temples and shrines he had built, are recorded in the Great Harris Papyrus.

Ramesses III was fatally wounded during a plot to kill him, hatched by one of his minor wives, Tiye. His death contributed to bringing Egypt into financial and social decline. Never again would the country be so powerful.

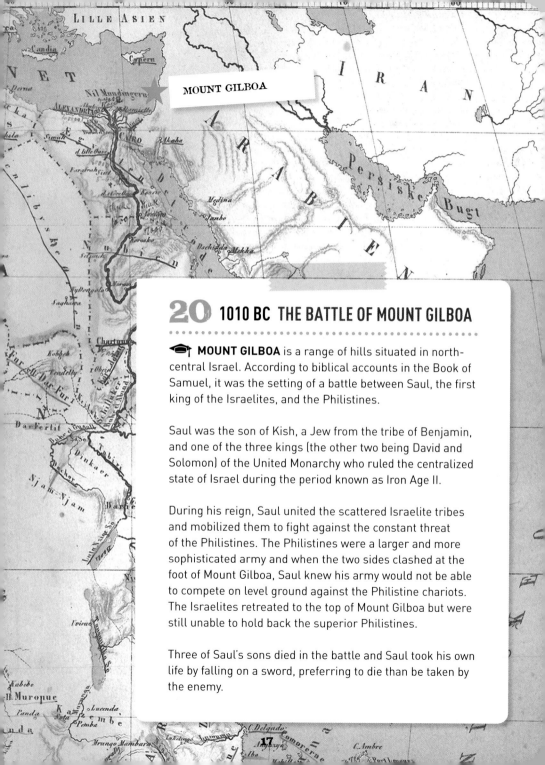

MOUNT GILBOA

20 1010 BC THE BATTLE OF MOUNT GILBOA

MOUNT GILBOA is a range of hills situated in north-central Israel. According to biblical accounts in the Book of Samuel, it was the setting of a battle between Saul, the first king of the Israelites, and the Philistines.

Saul was the son of Kish, a Jew from the tribe of Benjamin, and one of the three kings (the other two being David and Solomon) of the United Monarchy who ruled the centralized state of Israel during the period known as Iron Age II.

During his reign, Saul united the scattered Israelite tribes and mobilized them to fight against the constant threat of the Philistines. The Philistines were a larger and more sophisticated army and when the two sides clashed at the foot of Mount Gilboa, Saul knew his army would not be able to compete on level ground against the Philistine chariots. The Israelites retreated to the top of Mount Gilboa but were still unable to hold back the superior Philistines.

Three of Saul's sons died in the battle and Saul took his own life by falling on a sword, preferring to die than be taken by the enemy.

21 995 BC KING DAVID CAPTURES JERUSALEM

 **THE BIBLICAL KING DAVID** ruled Israel for 40 years (1010–970 BC). He was a skilled writer of psalms and a warrior who led his people to victory in numerous battles. Until recently, the only evidence for the existence of David was within the pages of the Bible. However, in 1993 a team of archeologists unearthed a piece of inscribed rock at Tel Dan in northern Galilee, which indicates that a King David almost certainly did exist during the relevant period.

Jerusalem is the capital city of Israel and is situated in the Judean Mountains between the Mediterranean Sea and the Dead Sea. During the biblical period of the Judges, it was a Jebusite city called Jebus. The Bible tells that David sent his troops to capture the city and the ancient fortress of Zion, and to establish Jerusalem as the capital of the Kingdom of Israel and the center of Jewish worship.

The Jebusites were not expelled from Jerusalem. On the contrary, they were treated fairly, employed as administrators, and enlisted into King David's army.

22 FAST FACT...

KING DAVID began life as a shepherd near Bethlehem.

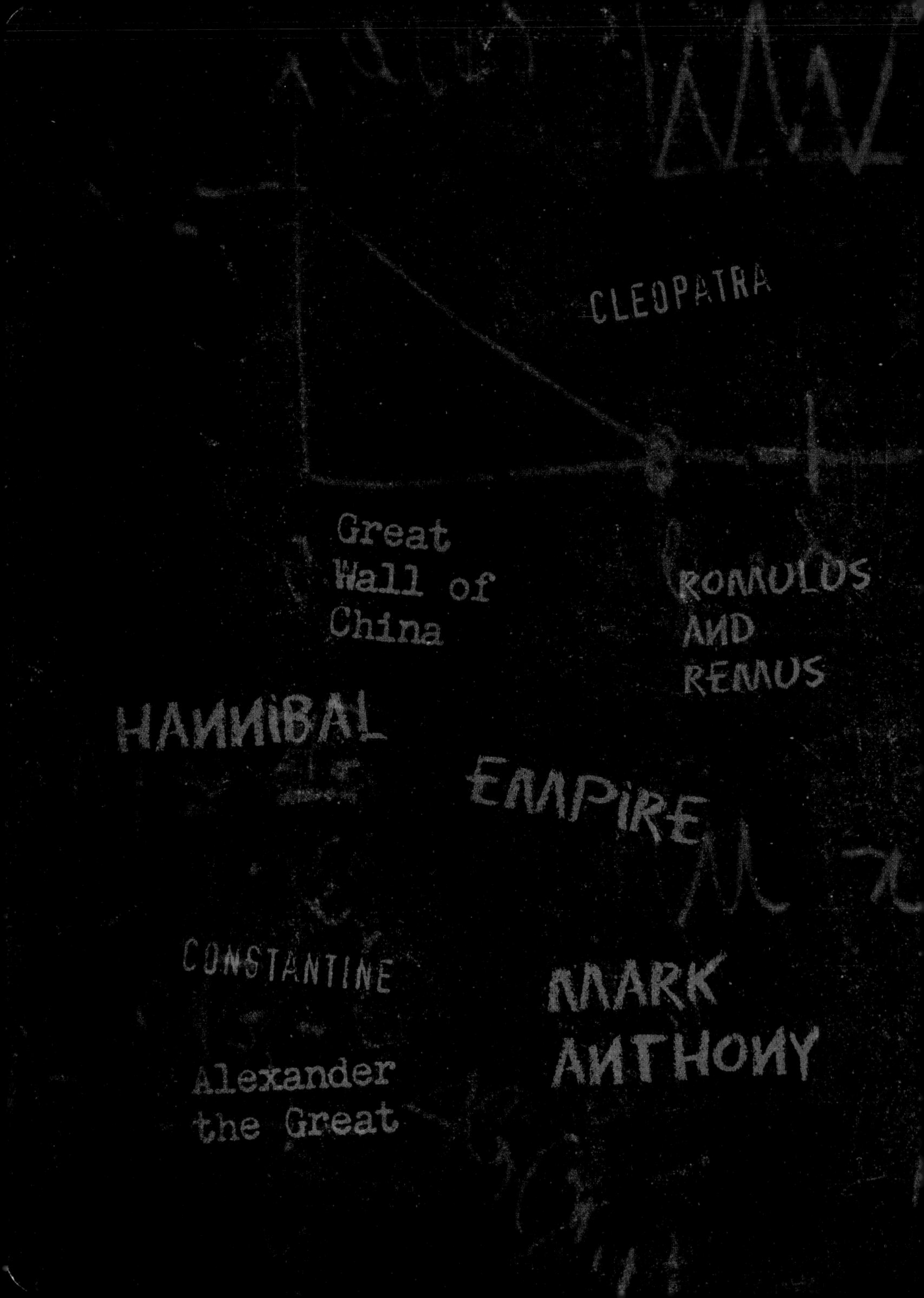

CLEOPATRA

Great
Wall of
China

ROMULUS
AND
REMUS

HANNIBAL

EMPIRE

CONSTANTINE

MARK
ANTHONY

Alexander
the Great

JULIUS CAESAR

OLYMPICS

Ancient History

SPARTACUS

SALAMIS

POMPEII

ROME

Boudicca

EUREKA!

23 776 BC THE FIRST OLYMPIC GAMES

🎓 **THE FIRST** recorded Olympic Games were held at Olympia (within the district of Elis in Southern Greece) in 776 BC. Held in honor of the Greek god Zeus, the Games were part of an important religious festival, and the Olympian site boasted a purpose-built temple, containing a 42 feet-high gold and ivory statue of the king of gods. The Games were also intended to help ease tensions between warring Greek city-states.

Male participants came from all over Greece to take part in running, wrestling, pentathlon, boxing, and equestrian events. Olympic victors were considered heroes who brought honor to their own city-states. They were crowned with an olive wreath and feted for the rest of their lives.

The Games took place every four years and the period between the Games was known as an Olympiad. The Olympiads were established as a unit of measuring time.

As the Romans gained power in Greece, the importance of the Games diminished. The last of the ancient Games were held in 393 AD, after which Emperor Theodosius I forbade all deity worshipping. The Olympic Games were not revived until 1896.

24 FAST FACT...

📖 **In 621 BC,** Draco, the lawgiver of Athens, decreed that the punishment for any crime was death. Since then, severe punishments have been called draconian.

Don't try this at home!

25 FAST FACT...

📖 **GREEK ATHLETE** Protesilaus hurled a discus an astonishing 152 feet in 600 BC. His record stood until 1928.

26 753 BC THE FOUNDING OF ROME

🎓 **THE FOUNDING OF ROME** is steeped in legend and mythology, the most deep-rooted being the story of Romulus and Remus. After being abandoned as babies, the twin brothers (who were descended from the Trojan, Aeneas) were found by a she-wolf, who nursed them until they were discovered by a shepherd, who then raised them as his own. When they became adults, the twins became determined to found a city on the Palatine Hill, the site where they were abandoned as babies. According to legend, the brothers fought and Remus was murdered by his brother, leaving Romulus to become the first king of Rome. The date traditionally given for the founding of the city is April 21, 753 BC. This date is still acknowledged and celebrated today.

Archeological evidence points towards the existence of two tribes of peoples, the Latins and the Sabines, who formed settlements on the Palatine Hill and the Quirinal. The two tribes joined forces to protect themselves from attack, and their combined success as traders and farmers explains how, from its very early origins, Rome was a rich city.

The statue in this painting shows the she-wolf suckling the babies Romulus and Remus

27 FAST FACT...

📖 **THE BATTLE** of Salamis (opposite) was the largest naval battle of ancient times, involving 1642 ships.

28 479 BC THE BATTLES OF SALAMIS AND PLATAEA

IN 480 BC, the Persian Empire (under the rule of Great King Xerxes) invaded mainland Greece, seeking revenge for the defeat suffered by the Persians in their first invasion of Greece in 490 BC.

The Battle of Salamis was fought in the straits between mainland Greece and the island of Salamis, near Athens. Although greatly outnumbered by the Persian fleet, which included hundreds of Egyptian, Phoenician and Ionian ships, the Greeks showed superior ship handling skills and secured a victory as the large Persian force struggled with the narrowness of the straits. At least 300 Persian ships were sunk or captured.

Xerxes retreated to Persia with what remained of his fleet, leaving his general, Mardonius, and a large army behind to try again the following year.

The Battle of Plataea took place in the summer of 479 BC near the city of Plataea in Boeotia. Again, it proved to be a decisive Greek victory. It is cited as being one of the most important battles in history, ensuring that the Greek culture and influence continued to grow and spread, shaping the course of European history.

29 FAST FACT...

IN 356 BC, Herostratus set fire to the Temple of Artemis just to get his name in the history books. It worked!

30 FAST FACT...

GREEK playwright Aeschylus died in 455 BC when an eagle dropped a tortoise on his head.

sorry!!!

31 336 BC ALEXANDER THE GREAT

ALEXANDER III of Macedon (or Alexander the Great as he is better known) was born in Pella, the capital of Macedonia, in 356 BC. He was educated in politics and the military and was tutored by the Greek philosopher, Aristotle.

In 336 BC, his father (Philip II of Macedon) was assassinated and Alexander took control of the warring Macedonian state. He inherited his father's military genius and under his leadership the Macedonian army swept through the Persian Empire, Egypt, Syria, and Asia Minor. In 331 BC he achieved his greatest victory in the Battle of Gaugamela, which led to the fall of the Achaemenid Empire. Over the course of eight years, Alexander expanded his empire across three continents and became a legend in his own lifetime. He was a generous and tolerant leader, respecting the cultures of every country he conquered.

32 FAST FACT...

IN 262 BC, Greek playwright Philemon died from laughing at one of his own jokes.

In 323 BC, Alexander travelled to Babylon to lay plans for the conquering of northern African. He fell ill with a fever and died in June the same year. His empire fell apart upon his death but his extension of Greek culture had a lasting effect upon the world.

33 221 BC THE GREAT WALL OF CHINA

THE GREAT WALL of China is the largest man-made structure in the world. Qin Shi Huangdi, ruler of the Qin Dynasty and the First Emperor of China, began construction of the wall in 221 BC. It was built to protect against invasion from neighboring states and as a symbol of the emperor's great power.

Work began (under the supervision of General Meng Tian) by connecting existing border walls. The section of the wall completed during the Qin Dynasty extended 2583 miles from Lintao to Liaodong. It travelled east to west through difficult terrain and even across the Yellow River. Thousands of workers lost their lives in the 10 years it took to build.

34 FAST FACT...

IN 213 BC, Emperor Qin Shi Huang ordered the burning of every book in China.

Many types of material were used in the construction of the wall, from mortar bricks and granite to mud and reeds. The wall was extended many times throughout subsequent dynasties, the last major work being done during the Ming Dynasty in around 1500 AD. The wall now measures 4163 miles in length and stretches across five provinces.

35 215 BC SPECIFIC GRAVITY DISCOVERED

SPECIFIC GRAVITY (or relative density) is the ratio of density of a substance compared to the density of the same unit volume of a reference substance (often water). It was discovered by the Greek mathematician Archimedes in 215 BC.

Born to a family of aristocrats in Syracuse, Sicily, in 287 BC, Archimedes studied in Alexandria and became the ancient world's greatest mathematician and geometer.

Archimedes' life was chronicled by various writers, such as Plutarch, who described him as having been a close relative of King Heiron II of Syracuse.

Legend has it that the king suspected a goldsmith had defrauded him by mixing less valuable silver into a gold crown. The king asked Archimedes to determine whether his suspicions were legitimate. Pondering upon the problem, Archimedes took a bath. As he got in, he noticed that water spilt over the edge and realized that the amount of water lost was equal in volume to the space his body occupied. He knew the principle could be applied to determine a mass of gold against a mass of silver. He was so overwhelmed by his discovery that he jumped out of the bath shouting "Eureka!" (I have found it!).

36 FAST FACT...

📖 *"Eureka" is the motto of the state of California and appears on the Great State Seal.*

37 202 BC THE BATTLE OF ZAMA

THE BATTLE OF ZAMA was fought in October 202 BC and marked the end of the Second Punic War.

Legendary Carthaginian general, Hannibal Barca (Rome's greatest enemy), clashed with the Roman army (led by Scipio Africanus, one of the greatest commanders in ancient military history) at Zama in North Africa.

Hannibal had already secured earlier victories against the Roman army, most spectacularly in Cannae, Italy, when he had led his army and an elephant corps over the Alps in a surprise attack. He was forced to return to his homeland when the Romans launched a counter invasion.

When the two sides met at Zama, they numbered around 35–40,000 troops each, plus Hannibal again had a large elephant corps. Hoping to defeat the Romans with the might of his elephants, Hannibal was outwitted by the Romans' superior tactics. The elephants panicked after Scipio ordered his trumpeters to sound their instruments, and the Romans took advantage of the resulting confusion to charge the Carthaginians.

Hannibal's defeat at Zama marked the end of the Carthaginian Empire and saw Rome at the pinnacle of its military powers.

38 89–84 BC THE FIRST MITHRIDATIC WAR

FOUGHT BETWEEN the ambitious King Mithridates of Pontus (in modern-day Turkey) and the Roman Republic, the first Mithridatic War began when Mithridates, in alliance with his son-in-law Tigranes of Armenia, invaded Roman provinces in Asia.

His occupation of Bithynia and Cappadocia was challenged by Lucius Cornelius Sulla, the governor of Cilicia, and he was ordered to withdraw and pay compensation. Mithridates refused to pay and, taking advantage of Sulla's preoccupation with the Social War in Italy, he pressed forward into Asia Minor, ordering the massacre of thousands of Italians in the area. He formed alliances with Athens and other Greek city-states and took control of the Black Sea and the Aegean.

Eventually, Rome raised an army against him, under the command of Sulla, and recaptured Athens before defeating Mithridates in the decisive battles of Chaerona and Orchomenus in central Greece.

The first Mithridatic War ended in 84 BC with the signing of the Treaty of Dardanus, the terms of which forced Mithridates to concede all captured provinces and to pay a fine to Rome.

39 FAST FACT...

AFTER THE DEFEAT of Spartacus' slave revolt against the Romans in 71 BC, 6600 of his followers were crucified.

LE SERMENT DE SPARTACVS

40 44 BC THE MURDER OF JULIUS CAESAR

GAIUS JULIUS CAESAR was a distinguished Roman general who rose through the ranks of Roman government to become a self-appointed dictator for life of the Roman Republic.

In 60 BC, Caesar was elected consul, the most coveted position within the government. Rome already had two consuls in the great generals Crassus and Pompey. To obtain a consulship of his own, Caesar had persuaded Crassus and Pompey to form a political alliance (the First Triumvirate).

41 FAST FACT...

WHEN WEALTHY Roman Marcus Licinius Crassus died in 53 BC, molten gold was poured down his throat as a symbol of his greed.

Caesar's continued appetite for achievement saw him conquer Gaul in 51 BC, build a bridge across the Rhine, and initiate the first expedition to Britain. These military successes upset the balance of power within the Triumvirate and, with the death of Crassus in 53 BC, Caesar went on to amass further power, eventually being declared *"dictator perpetuo"* by the Senate.

Fearing that Caesar was now in a position to overthrow the Senate, around 60 senators, or Liberators, plotted his death. On the Ides of March (March 15) 44 AD, the senators, led by Marcus Junius Brutus and Gaius Cassius Longinus, stabbed Caesar to death in the theater of Pompey.

Et tu, Brutus?

42 FAST FACT...

"Veni, vidi, vici" (I came, I saw, I conquered) – Julius Caesar (100–44 BC)

EARLY ROMAN EMPERORS

NAME	REIGN	DEATH
Augustus (63 BC–14 AD)	27 BC–14 AD	Natural causes
Tiberius (42 BC–37 AD)	14 AD–37 AD	Possibly assassinated
Caligula (12 AD–41 AD)	37 AD–41 AD	Assassinated
Claudius (10 BC–54 AD)	41 AD–54 AD	Poisoned
Nero (37 AD–68 AD)	54 AD–68 AD	Suicide
Galba (3 BC–69 AD)	68 AD–69 AD	Murdered
Otho (32 AD–69 AD)	January–April 69 AD	Suicide
Vitellius (15 AD–69 AD)	April–December 69 AD	Murdered
Vespasian (9 AD–79 AD)	69 AD–79 AD	Natural causes
Titus (39 AD–81 AD)	79 AD–81 AD	Plague
Domitian (51 AD–96 AD)	81 AD–96 AD	Assassinated
Nerva (30 AD–98 AD)	96 AD–98 AD	Natural causes
Trajan (53 AD–117 AD)	98 AD–117 AD	Natural causes
Hadrian (76 AD–138 AD)	117 AD–138 AD	Natural causes
Antoninus Pius (86 AD–161 AD)	138 AD–161 AD	Natural causes
Lucius Verus (130 AD–169 AD)	161 AD–169 AD	Plague
Marcus Aurelius (121 AD–180 AD) *(co-emperor with Lucius Verus)*	161 AD–180 AD	Natural causes
Commodus (161 AD–192 AD)	177 AD–192 AD	Assassinated
Pertinax (126 AD–193 AD)	January–March 193 AD	Murdered
Didius Julianus (133 D–193 AD)	March–June 193 AD	Executed

43 31 BC BATTLE OF ACTIUM

🎓 **THE BATTLE OF ACTIUM**, fought between Gaius Julius Octavius (Octavian) and allies Mark Anthony and Cleopatra, Queen of Egypt, was the decisive battle of the Roman Republic civil wars.

Since the assassination of Julius Caesar in 44 BC, relations between Octavius and Mark Anthony had been very uneasy. This was partly political and partly personal, as Anthony had abandoned his wife (Octavius's sister) to begin a relationship with Cleopatra. On September 2, 31 BC, the two Roman forces faced each other at Actium on the west coast of Greece.

44 FAST FACT...

📖 **CALIGULA'S** favorite horse had 18 servants. It was fed oats mixed with gold flakes and lived in a marble stable.

Octavius's fleet (under the excellent command of Marcus Agrippa) forced Mark Anthony's fleet out from the Gulf of Ambracia to take the advantage. Even with the support of Cleopatra's ships, Anthony's main fleet was quickly destroyed. He escaped to the south in his own ship.

The Battle of Actium marked the end of the Roman Republic and Octavius's victory saw him gain sole power over Rome and its provinces. The Roman Empire was born and Octavius was rewarded with the title "Augustus." Anthony and Cleopatra both committed suicide.

45 FAST FACT...

📖 **WHEN FATALLY ILL**, Emperor Vespasian (9–79 AD) was heard to say: *"Woe is me. I think I am becoming a god."*

Emperor Vespasian
(9–79 AD)

46 43 AD ROMAN INVASION OF BRITAIN

🎓 **ROMAN ARMIES** first came to Britain in 55 BC and 54 BC. Both expeditions were called off, however, due to political unrest in Gaul and other parts of the Roman Empire.

It was another 100 years before the Romans finally sailed the four legions from Boulogne to the Solent and landed at Richborough, Kent. The legions were led by Emperor Claudius and General Aulus Plautius. As a new Emperor, Claudius was anxious to prove himself, and a successful invasion of Britain would ensure the security of the western side of the Roman Empire. Britain was also rich in raw materials and agricultural land.

47 FAST FACT...

📖 **IN THE YEAR** 238 AD there were six different emperors of Rome.

Initial British resistance was led by the Catuvellauni tribe. They showed fierce courage but were soon defeated by the sophisticated Roman army.

Southern Britain fell to Roman rule first. Londinium (London) was founded and a network of roads built across the south. After crushing a revolt led by Boudicca of the Iceni tribe, the Romans eventually conquered the North. Forty-one years after the initial invasion, the whole of Britain came under Roman rule.

Boudicca's story was revived during the reign of Queen Victoria and many statues of her date from this time.

48 79 AD MOUNT VESUVIUS ERUPTS

MOUNT VESUVIUS is situated near to the city of Naples, Italy. On August 24, 79 AD, it erupted and spewed vast quantities of ash over the city of Pompeii and its smaller neighbors, Herculaneum and Stabiae. The inhabitants were suffocated and the towns left completely buried in volcanic ash and mud.

The eruption of Vesuvius was described in detail by Pliny the Younger, an eyewitness who was staying at his uncle's house in the town of Misenum, across the Bay of Naples from Pompeii. He described how, on the day of the eruption, a mushroom-shaped cloud of smoke appeared above Vesuvius. The volcanic column is thought to have reached 66,000 feet in height, with the ash and pumice raining down for almost 18 hours. Pliny the Younger described the aftermath thus: *"The sight that met our still-terrified eyes was a changed world, buried in ash like snow."*

49 FAST FACT...

DURING the 100 days of the opening games at the Roman Colosseum in 80 AD, over 5000 animals were killed.

50 FAST FACT...

ROMAN EMPEROR Elagabalus (218–222 AD) accidentally suffocated his dinner guests beneath a mass of rose petals, dropped from the ceiling.

51 FAST FACT...

THE FIRST NATION to make Christianity its official religion was Armenia, in 301 AD.

52 313 AD CONSTANTINE THE GREAT ADOPTS CHRISTIANITY

🎓 **EMPEROR CONSTANTINE** the Great (288–337 AD) succeeded his father (Chlorus) in 306 AD and began his rule amid much political upheaval.

53 FAST FACT...

📖 *"In hoc signo vinces"*
(In this sign shalt thou conquer)
– Emperor Constantine

54 FAST FACT...

📖 **THE GREATEST LIBRARY** of the ancient world, the Library of Alexandria, was burned to the ground by monks in 391 AD.

Believing himself to be the rightful emperor of the whole Western Roman Empire, Constantine prepared to advance upon Emperor Maxentius, who occupied Rome. In 312 AD, after conquering Northern Italy, Constantine met with Maxentius's troops by the Milvian Bridge just outside Rome. On the night before the battle, Constantine saw a flaming cross in the sky with the words *"by this sign you shall conquer."* Constantine took this as divine intervention and ordered his soldiers to display the first two Greek letters of Christ's name (XP) on their standards. Maxentius's army was defeated and Constantine's faith in Christianity was strengthened.

Constantine signed the Edict of Milan in 313 AD, which declared religious tolerance within the Roman Empire.

After defeating his last rival, Licinius, in the Battle of Chrysopolis in 324 AD, Constantine became sole emperor of the Roman Empire. He adopted Christianity as the state religion and thus changed the course of world history.

55 FAST FACT...

📖 **ST SIMEON STYLITES** of Syria (390–459 AD) lived alone on top of a pillar for 39 years.

56 FAST FACT...

📖 **FEROCIOUS WARRIOR** Attila the Hun died in 453 AD after getting a nosebleed on his wedding night.

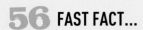

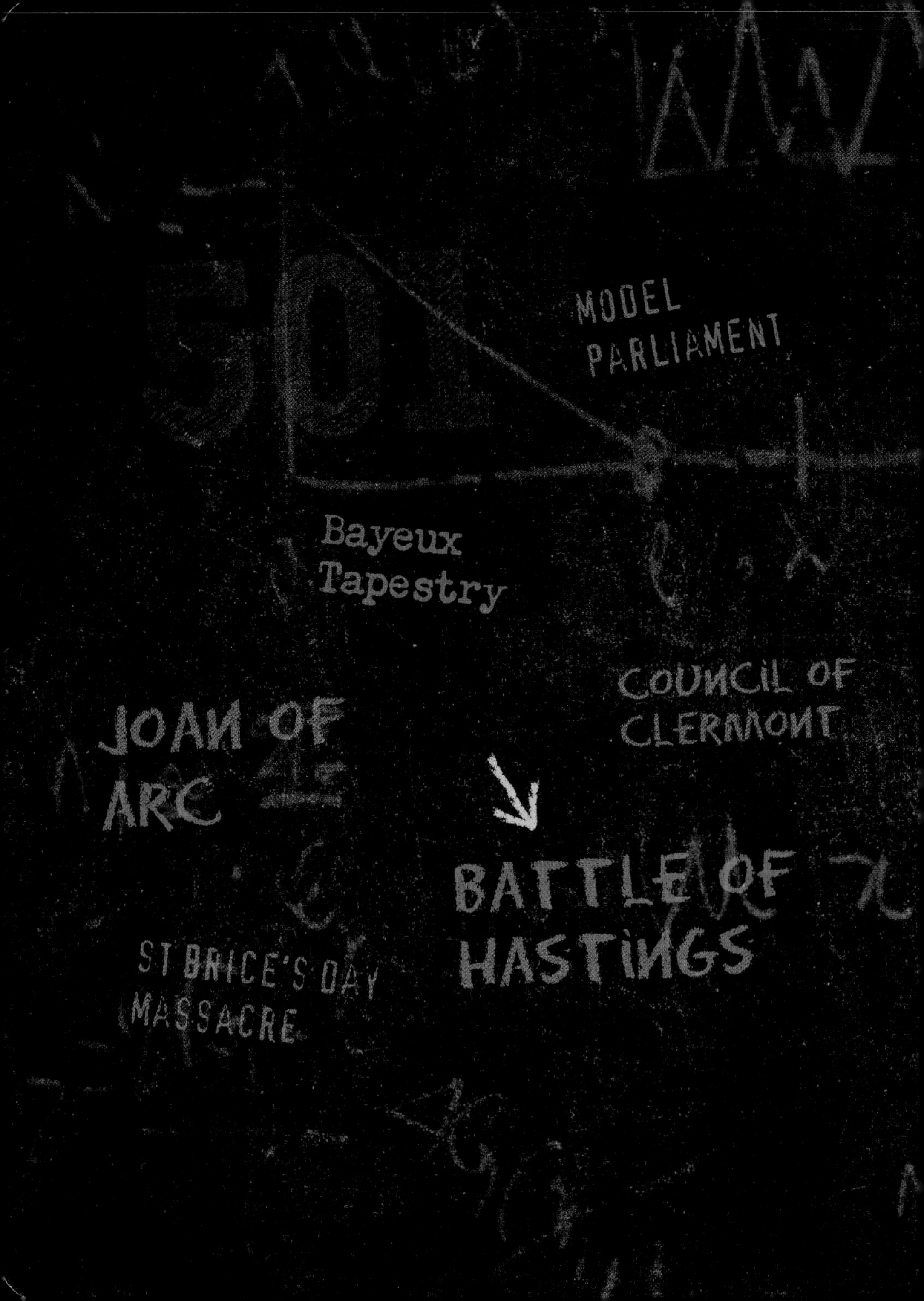

MODEL
PARLIAMENT

Bayeux
Tapestry

COUNCIL OF
CLERMONT

JOAN OF
ARC

↓

BATTLE OF
HASTINGS

ST BRICE'S DAY
MASSACRE

MUHAMMAD

FALL OF ROME

The Middle Ages

PRINTING PRESS

TANG DYNASTY

BLACK DEATH

MAGNA CARTA

CHARLEMAGNE

57 476 AD FALL OF THE ROMAN EMPIRE

🎓 **FROM AROUND 190 AD**, the Roman Empire had begun to weaken. Spread throughout western and eastern Europe, the empire was vast and becoming increasingly difficult to control centrally. There was widespread civil unrest and fighting within the Roman army, which led to there being no fewer than 23 different emperors between 211 AD and 284 AD.

By 284 AD, Emperor Diocletian had split the empire into eastern and western domains, each with its own ruler, but this did not ease the problems as he had hoped. The weakened empire was subject to continual invasion by tribes such as the Goths and the Vandals. The Roman army was spread too thin, had lost much of its military power, and become vulnerable. Rome itself was also suffering from increasing political and economic upheavals.

Romulus Augustulus was the last Roman Emperor of the west. In 476 AD, his reign was brought to an end when the German solider, Odovacar, took control over what remained of the Roman army in Italy and declared himself the first King of Italy. This event marked the end of the Roman Empire in the west and the beginning of the Dark Ages.

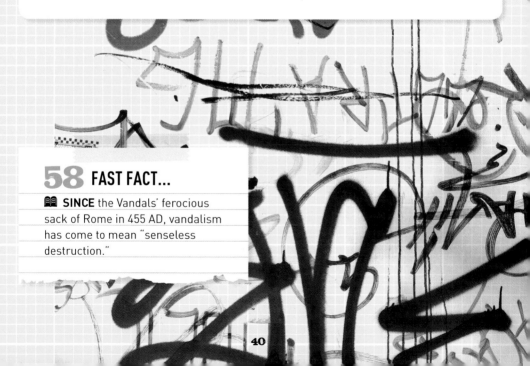

58 FAST FACT...

📖 **SINCE** the Vandals' ferocious sack of Rome in 455 AD, vandalism has come to mean "senseless destruction."

59 610 AD THE FIRST VISION OF MUHAMMAD

🎓 **MUHAMMAD** (or Muhamet) is the founder of Islam – one of the world's largest religions. He was born in 570 AD in the city of Mecca, now in Saudi Arabia.

Mecca was at the heart of Arabian religious culture and the place where, once a year, the various Arabian tribes would meet at an event known as the Hajj, to worship their various gods.

Muhammad was brought up by his uncle, Abu Talib, and spent his early adulthood involved with a group of Arab peoples known as the Hanefites. The Hanefites rejected idol worship in pursuit of a "true religion" and would retreat to the caves of Mecca in order to meditate. It was in one of these caves, on Mount Hera, that Muhammad had his first vision at the age of 40. As a result, he declared Allah as the one true God and himself to be the last prophet to mankind.

Muhammad was persecuted for his beliefs and for rejecting idol worshipping, instead preaching monotheism and predicting a Day of Judgment. Mecca cast him out, and in 622 AD he travelled to Medina (on a journey known as the Hijra) and became leader of the first Muslim community.

60 FAST FACT...

📖 **THE "TREATY OF ENDLESS PEACE"** between Byzantium and Persia in 533 AD lasted just seven years.

61 FAST FACT...

📖 **AT THE HEIGHT** of the Plague of Justinian (541–2 AD), between 5000 and 10,000 people were dying every day.

62 618 AD LI YUAN FIRST EMPEROR OF TANG DYNASTY

BORN IN 566 AD, Li Yuan (later known as Gaozu) was the first Emperor of the Chinese Tang Dynasty.

63 FAST FACT...

THE ONLY FEMALE emperor in China's history was Wu Zetian (690–705 AD).

During the Sui Dynasty (which began in 582 AD), Li Yuan was a governor, holding the title of Duke of Tang. He was cousin to Emperor Yang of the Sui Dynasty and in 613 AD he became a military general, gaining much experience and the support of his troops.

Around 616 AD, the Sui Dynasty began to weaken due to continued peasant revolts and Li Yuan, along with his son Li Shimin, took advantage of the situation to lead a rebellion against Emperor Yang. In June 618 AD, after Emperor Yang was killed by his chancellor, Li Yuan was proclaimed Emperor Gaozu. The Tang Dynasty was founded and Chang'an declared the capital city.

Under the ruling of the Tang Dynasty, China became one of the most powerful and successful countries in the world, economically, politically and culturally.

In 626 AD, Emperor Gaozu abdicated from the throne in favor of his son, Li Shimin, and died at the Tai'an Palace in 635 AD.

64 FAST FACT...

IN 793 AD, a band of Vikings sacked the monastery at Lindisfarne, England. The scholar Alciun described the events as follows: *"Never before has such terror appeared in Britain as we have now suffered from a pagan race...The heathens poured out the blood of saints around the altar, and trampled on the bodies of the saints in the temple of God, like dung in the streets."*

65 800 AD CORONATION OF CHARLEMAGNE THE GREAT

🎓 **WHEN HIS FATHER,** Pepin the Short, died in 768 AD, Charlemagne (or Charles the Great as he was also known) took over as ruler of the Franks alongside his brother Carloman. He became the sole King of the Franks three years later when Carloman died.

66 FAST FACT...

📖 **AFTER** he died in 814 AD, Emperor Charlemagne's mummified body was placed on the royal throne, where it remained until 1215.

Charlemagne ruled the Franks for 47 years, gaining the reputation of being a formidable warrior and a generous and outstanding leader. He had close relations with the church, wishing to extend and protect Christendom, and he harbored ambitions to re-establish the power of the city of Rome. He spent almost 32 years of his reign in the conquering and conversion of the Pagan Saxons.

In 799 AD, Pope Leo III sought refuge from Charlemagne after being greatly troubled by anti-papist factions. Hoping to help restore peace, Charlemagne escorted the Pope back to Rome. On Christmas Day 800 AD, Charlemagne was kneeling during mass in St Peters when Pope Leo suddenly placed a golden crown on his head and declared him Augustus, Emperor of the Romans. This act saw the restoration of the Roman Empire in the west.

67 FAST FACT...

📖 **THE FIRST RECORDED FLIGHT** was by Abbas Ibn Firnas in 875 AD. He launched his glider from a mountain top near Cordoba, Spain.

68 FAST FACT...

📖 **POPE FORMOSUS**, who died in 896 AD, was dug up a year later and put on trial for crimes committed during his lifetime.

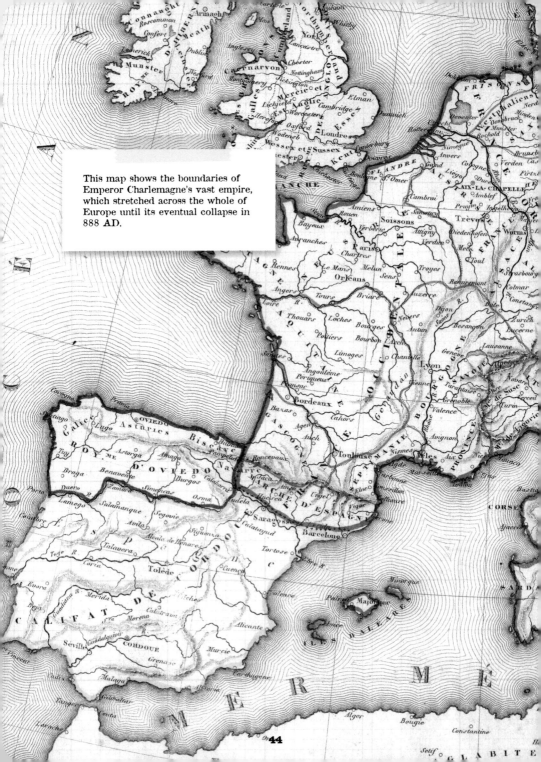

This map shows the boundaries of
Emperor Charlemagne's vast empire,
which stretched across the whole of
Europe until its eventual collapse in
888 **AD**.

EMPIRE
de
CHARLEMAGNE
PAR
A.H. Dufour

Myriamètres

Lieues de 25 au Degré

Milles d'Allemagne

MER BALTIQUE

POMERANIENS

PRUSSIENS

S l a v e s

POLACY
ou POLONAIS

Ilerich

Obotrites

Rewik

Wilziens

Velatabes

Aliens

Magdebourg

Sal-zao

Nord

Weissenfels

THURINGE

NE

Bamberg

NORDGAU

Dingelling

Pforing

bourg

Inspruck

Tirol

Botzen

Trente

Marche

Aquileja

Padoue

Mantoue

VENISE

RAVENNE

Ferrare

Bologne

rence

Sienne

Viterbe

Rome

Gaete

Capoue

Naples

Salerne

SICILE

Palerme

Messine

Reggio

Enna

Syracuse

Pantellerie

Malte

CRETE

Magdebourg

Morabes

Lusiziens

Erc. Geb.

Prague

Bohemien

Wissehrad

Alteich

Passau

Linz

Monsec

Salzbourg

Sarour

Faviana

Vienne

Baden

MARCHE ORIENTALE

PANNONIE

Comageni

Neutra

Hainburg

Obotrites

Res. ou camp du Khakan

Bude

Tolna

Drave R.

Peau

Cilli

ESCLAVONIE

Save R.

Sirmium

CROATIE
des Grecques

Narenta

Belgrade

Schabacs

SERVIE

Orschova

ROY.Me DE BULGARIE

Nicopoli

Silistri

Missivria

Batcan

Andrinople

GALITCHIE

Crapacks

Danaster R.

KHAZARS

Boug R.

Bong R.

HONGROIS

Theiss R.

Maros

Pruth R.

Sereth

Tiras

EMPIRE DES AVARES

EMPIRE DES BULGARES

Danube

PONT-EUXIN

Philippopoli

THRACE

Ousscup

Traganopolis

Constantinop

Erakli

Lampsaqui

Pergame

Adramitti

Smyrne

Sart

MYSIE

Lydie

Antiochi

Carie

Halicarna

Rhod

CRETE

69 962 AD OTTO THE GREAT AND THE HOLY ROMAN EMPIRE

🎓 **IN THE 100 YEARS** after the death of Charlemagne the Great, the title of Holy Roman Emperor held increasingly little sway. It was not until 962 AD, when the German King Otto I (also known as Otto the Great) persuaded Pope John XII to crown him, that the role of Holy Roman Emperor was truly revived. The coronation marked the establishment of an uninterrupted line of Christian emperors in the west that continued for more than eight centuries.

Otto I had succeeded his father (Henry I) as Duke of Saxony in 936 AD. He quickly established his military prowess during the Ducal Rebellions in 941, and again in 951 when he conquered Italy and declared himself king. He defeated the Magyars in the Battle of Lechfield in 955, bringing peace to his empire. After establishing the Church-State alliance, Otto I had the power to appoint church officials.

When he was crowned Roman Emperor, Otto also became head of the Church, and he imposed the rule that a pope could not be elected without the approval of the emperor. Otto I is known as being one of the greatest of Saxon rulers.

Eric the Red, who discovered and named Greenland

70 FAST FACT...

📖 **ABDUL KASSAM ISMAEL**, a 10th-century Persian ruler, traveled with 400 camels carrying all 117,000 books in his library.

71 FAST FACT...

📖 **THE WORLD'S FIRST** paper money was issued in China in 960 AD.

72 FAST FACT...

📖 **THE WORST POPE** in history was John XII (955–964 AD). He drank toasts to the devil, gambled, stole, murdered, and committed adultery and incest.

73 FAST FACT...

📖 **GREENLAND** was discovered by the Viking Eric the Red (950–1003). He gave it that name not because it was green, but to attract other settlers.

74 1002 ST BRICE'S DAY MASSACRE

🎓 **ETHELRED II** (Ethelred the Unready) was the Saxon King of England from 978–1016. He became king at the age of 10 after his half-brother (King Edward) was murdered by their step-mother, Elfthryth. Due to the circumstances of his succession, Ethelred was always an unpopular ruler.

75 FAST FACT...

📖 **IN 990,** a law was passed called "The Truce of God," banning battles between Wednesday evening and Monday morning.

At the time of Ethelred's rule, England had long been troubled by continual invasions by the Danish Vikings. An uneasy truce had been agreed between Ethelred and Danish King Sweyn "Forkbeard." Ethelred paid Sweyn protection money and held some Danish hostages as an insurance against a Viking invasion.

However, Sweyn was not the only Viking threat. Many Danes had already settled in England and, fearing an uprising, Ethelred made the drastic decision to slaughter all Danes on English soil.

On St Brice's Day (named after St Brice, Bishop of Tours) November 13, 1002, the massacre took place. Whole Viking villages were decimated, and the church of St Frideswide's in Oxford was burned down when fleeing Danes sought sanctuary there.

King Edmund II of England, who met an unfortunate end!

The massacre, not surprisingly, enraged the Danes and led to a full-scale Viking invasion of England the following year.

76 FAST FACT...

📖 **IN 1016,** King Edmund II of England was killed while seated on the toilet.

77 1066 THE BATTLE OF HASTINGS

🎓 **THE BATTLE OF HASTINGS** took place on the morning of October 14, 1066 at Senlac Hill near Hastings, England. It was fought between the English army under King Harold II and the Norman-French army under Duke William II of Normandy.

Harold claimed the throne in the January of 1066 when his predecessor, Edward the Confessor, died. It is thought that William of Normandy had been promised the crown and on hearing that Harold had taken the throne, he prepared to invade England and take the crown for himself.

78 FAST FACT...

📖 **WHEN WILLIAM** the Conqueror died in 1087, his decomposing body swelled up with gas. On the day of his funeral, his stomach exploded.

William gathered his forces from around France, Germany, and even Italy. With a heavily armored, highly trained cavalry, he set sail for England, landing at Pevensey Bay on 1 October 1066. Harold, although expecting the invasion, was unprepared, having fought off a Viking attack at Stamford Bridge only three weeks earlier.

The depleted English army – consisting entirely of infantry – was defeated by the Normans, and Harold was killed by an arrow through the eye. The Duke of Normandy was crowned King William "the Conqueror."

The Battle of Hastings was the last time the British Isles were successfully invaded by a foreign force. The battle is recorded in the famous Bayeux Tapestry.

This section of the Bayeux Tapestry shows King Harold (far right) being killed by an arrow through his eye.

hARO L

79 1095 THE COUNCIL OF CLERMONT

THE COUNCIL OF CLERMONT was an assembly for church reform that consisted of around 300 laymen and ecclesiastics. It was called by Pope Urban II and took place between November 18–28, 1095 in Clermont, France.

The Byzantine Emperor, Alexius I Comnenus, had asked the Pope for aid from the west earlier that year, to help the Greeks in their struggle against the Muslim Turks who had taken over large parts of Asia Minor.

Towards the end of the assembly on November 27, after speaking on various church reform matters such as simony, clerical marriage and the continued ex-communication of King Philip of France for adultery, Pope Urban eventually addressed the problems in the east.

In a rousing speech, which was to initiate the First Crusade, he urged all the French knights at Clermont to rise up and take arms to rescue Palestine from the Turks.

Pope Urban ended his speech with the words *"Deus Vult!"* (God wills it!). These words became the battle cry of the crusaders during the religious wars in the Holy Land that followed.

80 FAST FACT...

📖 **AFTER THE DEATH** of the Spanish knight El Cid in 1099, his soldiers strapped his corpse to his horse so he could lead them into battle one last time.

81 FAST FACT...

📖 **IN THE 1130'S**, Chinese rebels dressed monkeys in straw and set fire to them to cause trouble in the imperial camp.

82 FAST FACT...

📖 **DURING THE 1148** siege of Damascus by the crusaders, a female Arab archer killed the crusaders' commander, winning the battle.

83 FAST FACT...

📖 **IN 1212**, a children's crusade set off for the Holy Land. The 7000 children died of disease and starvation before reaching Jerusalem.

84 1215 MAGNA CARTA SIGNED

THE MAGNA CARTA is an English Charter that was signed by the barons of medieval England and a reluctant King John of England on June 15, 1215, at Runnymede, Surrey. The King signed the charter under duress, as the laws it contained reduced his authority over his subjects and the powers he held as king.

King John had long been in dispute with the barons over his methods of ruling the country. He had imposed unwanted taxes, angered the Catholic Church and lost territory in northern France.

85 FAST FACT...

"To no man will we sell, or deny, or delay, right or justice."
– Magna Carta, 1215

86 FAST FACT...

QUEEN MARGARET of Scotland never set foot on Scottish soil. She was on her way there from Norway in 1290, but died en route from the effects of seasickness. She was eight years old.

The barons rebelled against the king and in May 1215 they took up arms and captured London. The contents of the Magna Carta were drawn up by one of the most powerful English Barons, the Archbishop Stephen Langton, and the king was left with no choice but to sign it.

King John signs the Magna Carta

The main clauses of the charter stated that all "freemen" could only be punished by the laws of the land (this led to trial by jury). The Church and the election of bishops were free from royal intervention and taxes could only be levied by consent of Parliament.

The Magna Carta influenced many later legal documents, such as the United States Constitution.

87 1295 MODEL PARLIAMENT

🎓 **THE ENGLISH PARLIAMENT**
set up by King Edward I of England on November 13, 1295, was called the Model Parliament as it became the blueprint for all subsequent parliaments. It was the first to include representatives outside the clergy and aristocracy.

The King invited representatives from each county and borough, with the counties sending two knights, the boroughs two burgesses (local officials) and there being two citizens from every city. The King stated, *"what touches all, should be approved of all, and it is also clear that common dangers should be met by measures agreed upon in common."*

King Edward I was also known as Edward Longshanks, meaning "long legs", as he was over 6 feet tall

The assembled Commons were made up of 219 town representatives and 49 lords and clergy.

The King's main aim in summoning the parliament was to raise much-needed money for his military campaigns in Scotland, Wales and France and to gain the support of his country. In return for agreeing to the King's request for extra taxes, the Commons took the opportunity to air its various grievances and asked for them to be addressed. Negotiations between Crown and Commons began, and the true concept of a modern parliament was born.

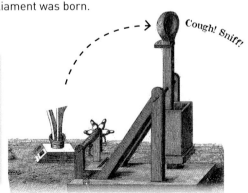

Cough! Sniff!

88 FAST FACT...

📖 **IN 1347**, a Mongolian army tried to spread the plague to the enemy city of Caffa by catapulting plague victims over the city walls.

89 1348–1350 THE BLACK DEATH

THE BLACK DEATH (or Bubonic Plague) is thought to have originated in the Far East in around 1347, and quickly spread along major trade routes.

It reached England in the summer of 1348 with devastating effects. The disease was borne by bacteria and was carried in the blood of fleas that lived on rats. The filthy, littered streets and overcrowded conditions of medieval English cities provided the perfect environment for the rat population to flourish.

Once bitten by an infected flea, a painful death followed within three days. Victims displayed fist-sized red swellings called buboes, which later turned black and gave the disease its name.

Over the course of two years the Plague killed 30–40% of the population, with entire communities being wiped out. With the population nearly halved, there was not enough labor to work the land or tend to livestock.

As a result, the entire economic system changed. Increased wages and prices forced the movement of labor around the country. Many believe this led to the Peasant Revolt of 1381.

The council held by the rats, a scene from the fables of La Fontaine.

90 FAST FACT...

ONE PREVENTATIVE MEASURE against the plague was drinking a cup of your own urine twice a day.

91 1368 EMPEROR HONG-WU ESTABLISHES MING DYNASTY

THE MING DYNASTY ruled China from 1368–1644, from the collapse of the Yuan Dynasty up to the establishment of the Qing Dynasty.

During the latter years of the Mongol Yuan Dynasty rule, tensions had been steadily growing between the Mongols and the Chinese, which eventually led to a peasant revolt led by Zhu Yuanzhang.

Zhu grew up an orphan in a Buddhist monastery and was schooled in politics by Confucian scholars. He became a strong rebel leader and after overthrowing the Yuan Dynasty, he became one of only two dynastic founders who came from peasant stock. In 1368, Zhu founded the Ming Dynasty, with Nanjing as its capital, and gave himself the title Emperor Hong-Wu.

The Ming Dynasty was a period of massive cultural and industrial growth. The porcelain industry grew to huge proportions and the iron industry flourished; agriculture improved; food supply increased; and the population doubled. Foreign trade expanded and a vast army and prestigious naval force were built.

Joan of Arc is a Catholic saint and is considered a national heroine of France

92 1429 JOAN OF ARC ENDS THE SIEGE OF ORLEANS

JOAN OF ARC (or The Maid of Orleans) was a peasant girl born around the year 1412 in the village of Domremy, eastern France.

At the age of about 12, Joan began to hear voices, which she claimed were from God, telling her to free her country from English domination. France was at the time embroiled in the Hundred Years War; a series of conflicts between England and France to lay claim to the French throne. By 1415, the English occupied much of northern France following their victory at Agincourt.

In March 1429 Joan travelled to Chinon to convince the Dauphin of France (Charles VII) of her calling. Inspired by her claims, Charles allowed Joan to lead the French forces to retake Orleans, which had been under siege by the English since the previous October.

After only nine days, Joan managed to lift the siege. This astonishing victory over the English marked a turning point in the Hundred Years War and led to several more French victories and the crowning of Charles VII as King of France.

Joan was later captured by the Burgundians and burnt at the stake at the age of 19. She was beatified in 1909 and remains a national heroine of France.

93 1450 GUTENBERG'S PRINTING PRESS

BEFORE THE INVENTION of the printing press in 1450, books and manuscripts were written by hand. This was obviously an expensive and very time-consuming process, which put the written word out of reach for the ordinary layman. By the thirteenth century, the import of block-printed books and cheaper paper from China began to revolutionize the production of books and documents. However, the woodcuts used for block-printing were highly perishable and a new block had to be cut for each new impression. With the increase in literacy and a greater reliance on written records, a less costly and more efficient method of printing needed to be found.

Born in 1398 in Mainz, Germany, Johannes Gutenberg, a goldsmith and stonecutter, had long been experimenting with the techniques of printing. Relying on investments from business associates, Gutenberg created the world's first movable type. Individual letters were carved in relief on metal alloy blocks, which could easily be moved to form whole pages of text and could be reused time and time again.

The first book printed using this new method was the Gutenberg Bible, of which 200 copies were produced.

94 FAST FACT...

BEFORE PAPER, many written documents were printed on vellum, made from the skin of a young animal.

95 1453 FALL OF CONSTANTINOPLE

🎓 **ON APRIL 6, 1453,** the Ottoman Empire, led by Sultan Mehmed II, laid siege to the Byzantine capital of Constantinople. The siege lasted until May 29, 1453, when the city finally fell to the Ottomans.

Employing a vast army of over 80,000 troops, Mehmet II used huge cannons (including one named Basilica that was 27 feet long) to blast through the walls of the heavily fortified city. He also built a huge fleet to take control of the surrounding sea and stationed these ships in the Golden Horn and off the Marmora shore.

96 FAST FACT...

📖 **IN 1491,** a Swiss court sentenced a chicken to death for laying a brightly colored egg.

The defending army, under Byzantine Emperor Constantine XI, consisted of only around 7000 troops, but they valiantly defended their city, quickly rebuilding walls between assaults. Constantine had also ordered an enormous chain to be placed across the entrance to the Golden Horn, preventing the entry of Ottoman ships.

Despite all efforts by the Byzantines, an all-out offensive beginning on May 29 saw the Ottomans breach the weaker walls and finally they entered the city. The fall of Constantinople marked the end of the Roman Empire.

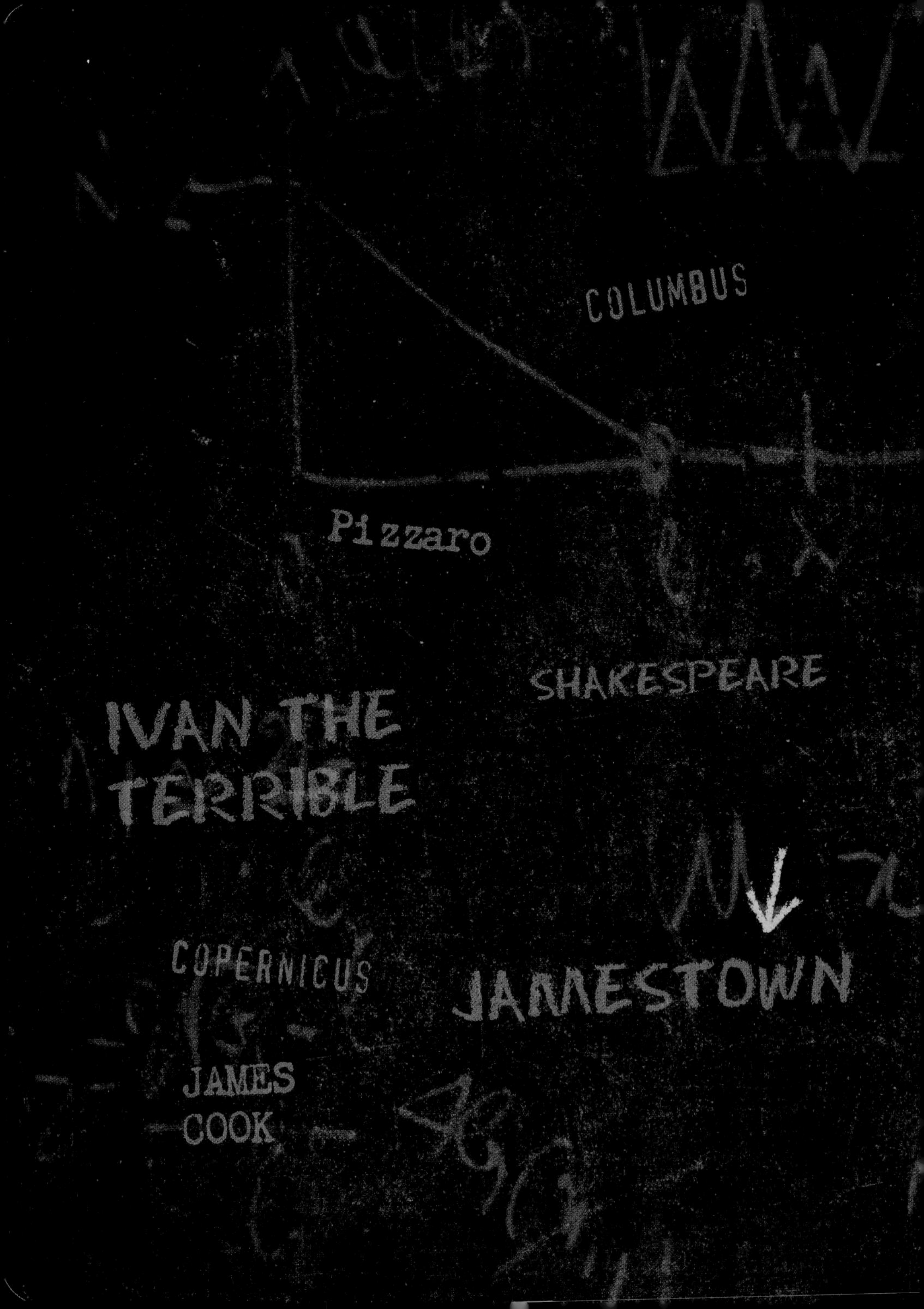

COLUMBUS

Pizzaro

SHAKESPEARE

IVAN THE
TERRIBLE

COPERNICUS

JAMESTOWN

JAMES
COOK

NEW ZEALAND

→ PIRATES

New Worlds

AUSTRALIA

CIVIL
WAR

PIRATES

GUNPOWDER
PLOT

THE
MAYFLOWER

THE EAST
INDIA
COMPANY

97 1493 COLUMBUS DISCOVERS THE NEW WORLD

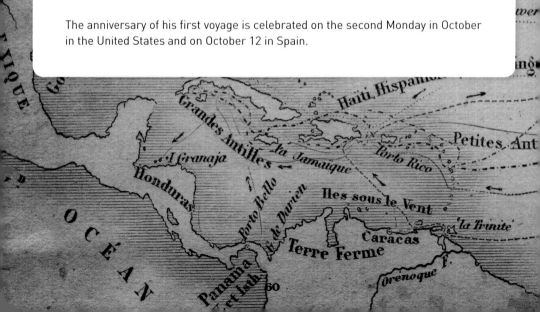

FINANCED by Queen Isabella of Spain, Christopher Columbus set sail from mainland Spain on August 3, 1492 in search of a western trade route from Europe to the spice-rich Asia. He commanded three ships: the *Nina*, the *Pinta* and the *Santa Maria*, and captained the *Santa Maria* himself.

On October 12, he landed in the Bahamas. Thinking he was in East Asia, he referred to the natives he found there as *"Indios."* He named the island San Salvador and claimed it for Spain.

He reached Cuba on October 28, mistakenly believing he had found China, and then in December he landed his ships in Hispaniola, thinking it may be Japan.
On Christmas Day, the *Santa Maria* ran aground and Columbus took over as captain of the *Nina.*

Columbus never achieved his original goal of reaching Asia via a westerly sea route, but over the course of his life he led other successful expeditions to the New World, discovering the Gulf of Mexico, the South and Central Americas and the Caribbean islands.

The anniversary of his first voyage is celebrated on the second Monday in October in the United States and on October 12 in Spain.

98 1494 THE TREATY OF TORDESILLAS

IN 1493, following the first voyage and discoveries of Christopher Columbus, and to avoid confusion over territorial claims, Pope Alexander VI of Spain issued a decree that divided the non-Christian world between Spain and Portugal. He established an imaginary north-south demarcation line through the Atlantic, 298 miles west of Cape Verde. All unclaimed lands to the west of this line would belong to Spain and all those to the right to Portugal.

99 FAST FACT...

IN 1502, Christopher Columbus became the first ever European to taste chocolate.

This decision angered the Portuguese, who argued that the Pope's dividing line conflicted with previous agreements. In the spring of 1494, officials from Spain and Portugal met in the Spanish town of Tordesillas to decide upon a satisfactory solution for both nations.

On June 7, the two parties compromised and signed the Treaty of Tordesillas. It was agreed that the line of demarcation be moved to a position 1100 miles west of Cape Verde. The Treaty resulted in Portugal gaining a large part of Brazil while Spain could put claim to the majority of the New World.

Spain prospered as a result of the Treaty, sending numerous expeditions into South America and establishing a large empire.

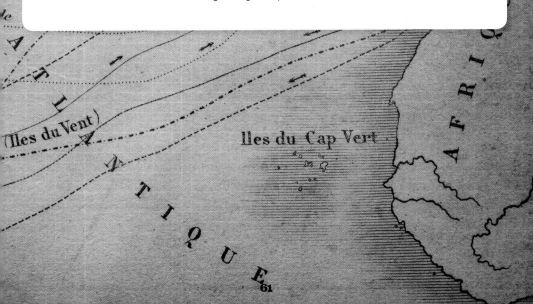

100 1498 VASCO DE GAMA REACHES INDIA

🎓 **IN JULY 1497,** Portuguese explorer Vasco de Gama set sail from Lisbon, Portugal hoping to find a sea route to India and gain access to the profitable trade in spices from the Far East.

De Gama capitalized on Portugal's expertise in maritime exploration, made possible by the efforts of Prince Henry the Navigator of Portugal, by bringing together talented mapmakers, geographers and navigators. He was also able to learn from the experiences of earlier explorers. Bartholomew Diaz had discovered the Cape of Good Hope in 1488, proving the Indian and Atlantic oceans were not land-locked, and Pedro da Covilha had traveled overland to India and mapped out the East African and Indian coastlines.

101 FAST FACT...

📖 When Spanish conquistador Hernan Cortes landed in Mexico in 1518, the native Aztecs thought he was a god.

Ten months after leaving Portugal, de Gama reached Calicut, India on May 20, 1498. He was met with hostility from the Muslim merchants who saw him as their rival. Despite this setback, de Gama set sail for home on August 29, 1498 with a valuable cargo of spices. After contending with hostile weather conditions and losing half his crew, de Gama finally arrived back in Portugal in September 1499 to a hero's welcome.

102 FAST FACT...

📖 **IN THE PRINCE** (1513), Niccolo Machiavelli wrote: *"It is much safer for a prince to be feared than loved."*

Steel engraving of philosopher
Niccolo Machiavelli (1429–1527)

103 1519–24 CORTES CONQUERS MEXICO

SPANISH CONQUISTADOR Hernando Cortes was born in 1485 in Medellin, western Spain. As a young man he traveled to the Americas to make his fortune, and in 1511 he joined forces with explorer Diego Velazquez de Cuellar to conquer Cuba. Velazquez was made governor of the island and in 1518 he agreed to fund Cortes on an expedition to Mexico.

However, there was growing animosity between the two men and, mistrusting Cortes's motives, Velazquez recalled the expedition at the last moment. Cortes ignored the order and in an act of mutiny set sail for Mexico.

Hernando Cortes (1485–1547)

After landing on the continent with an army of around 500 men, Cortes allied himself with some of the indigenous people. On arriving in Cholula, the second largest city in Mexico, and perhaps fearing a native rebellion, Cortes ordered the slaughter of hundreds of unarmed citizens. He journeyed on to the Aztec capital of Tenochtitan, hiring more soldiers en route, and in 1521, after a three-month siege, the city fell. The new settlement, Mexico City, became the capital of Spanish America.

104 FAST FACT...

DURING THE REIGN of Henry VIII of England (1509–1547), around 70,000 people were executed.

105 FAST FACT...

FERDINAND MAGELLAN'S 1521 voyage may have been the first to circumnavigate the world – but Magellan himself died en route.

106 FAST FACT...

HENRY VIII'S second wife, Anne Boleyn (c.1504–1536), was said to have had 11 fingers and 3 breasts.

107 1520 SULEIMAN I ASCENDS THE THRONE

SULEIMAN I was born in 1494 in the city of Trabzon, on the Black Sea coast of Turkey. He was the son of Selim I, Sultan of the Ottoman Empire from 1512–1520. Upon the death of his father, Suleiman took the throne and became the tenth Sultan of the Ottoman Empire. His reign was the longest in Ottoman history, lasting from 1520 to his death in 1566.

Known variously as "Suleiman the Great" and "The Lawgiver," his reign brought the Ottoman Empire to the peak of its powers. He was inspired by Alexander the Great's vision of a world empire and led successful military campaigns to conquer Christian strongholds in Asia, Africa and Europe. His great Ottoman fleet ruled the seas from the Mediterranean to the Persian Gulf.

He was an educated man and an accomplished poet whose patronization of the arts and culture saw the empire produce a magnificent abundance of literature and art. He initiated positive changes within the systems of law, education and taxation, and brought great wealth to the empire by building fortresses, mosques, bridges and aqueducts.

Suleiman's Mosque
in Sultanahmet District
(Istanbul, Turkey)

108 1521 MARTIN LUTHER INAUGURATES REFORMATION

MARTIN LUTHER was born in 1483 in the town of Eisleben, Saxony (modern Germany), which was part of the Holy Roman Empire and under the Catholic rule of the Pope. Luther's religious feelings deepened while at law school in 1505, when he narrowly missed being struck by lightening. As a result of this near-death experience he entered a monastery, where he struggled to reconcile his spiritual beliefs with those of the monks. When he took a doctorate in theology at Wittenberg University, he began to read the Scriptures in great depth.

He began to speak out against church practices, such as the selling of indulgences, and in October 1517 he accused the Roman Catholic Church of heresy upon heresy when he nailed his *95 Theses* to the church door at Wittenberg. This act is cited by historians as being the starting point for the Protestant Reformation.

Luther's Protestant views were condemned by Pope Leo X and on 3 January 1521 he was excommunicated.

Luther produced an impressive body of writings and continued to preach his Protestant views. In 1535, he published a German translation of the Bible, which was widely distributed thanks to Gutenberg's printing press.

109 FAST FACT...

"For, where God built a church, there the devil would also build a chapel.... In such sort is the devil always God's ape."
– Martin Luther (1566)

Martin Luther burning the papal bull of excommunication in an act of defiance.

110 1532 CONQUEST OF THE INCAS BY PIZARRO

🎓 **SPANISH CONQUISTADOR** Francisco Pizarro was born in 1474 in the Spanish town of Trujillo.

In 1524 and 1526, inspired by Cortes's conquering of Mexico and hearing rumors of bountiful riches to be found in Peru, Pizarro organized two expeditions to conquer the Incan Empire. Both attempts failed as a result of unfavorable weather conditions and hostile natives. Despite being ordered by the governor of Panama to call off the expeditions, Pizarro remained determined and, after eventually reaching northern Peru and finding friendly natives and an abundance of gold, silver and other treasures, he returned to Spain to seek the king's permission to launch a third expedition.

With his authority over the expedition assured, Pizarro sailed from Panama in late 1530. This time Pizarro achieved his goal. Overcoming native resistance, he founded San Miguel de Piura, the first Spanish settlement in Peru, and went on to capture Atahualpa (the Incan Emperors) during the Battle of Cajamarca in 1532. Pizarro had Atahualpa executed in 1533 and took the Incan capital of Cuzco later that year, putting an end to the Incan Empire. He later established the new capital city of Lima.

111 FAST FACT...

📖 **FRANCISCO PIZARRO** conquered the mighty Incan empire with just 180 men, 27 horses and a cannon.

112 FAST FACT...

📖 **IN 16TH-CENTURY MEXICO,** the Aztecs fed the bodies of their sacrificial victims to the snakes that guarded their temples.

113 1543 COPERNICUS'S THEORY

🎓 POLISH ASTRONOMER

Nicolaus Copernicus is the founder
of modern astrology.

He developed an interest in the science
in his youth and in 1530 he wrote his
controversial work, *De Revolutionibus*.
His paper challenged the widely
accepted Ptolemiac theory of the
universe, which stated that the Earth
lay at the center of the universe with
the sun, the moon, and the known
planets revolving around it in orbit.

Nicolaus Copernicus
(1473–1543)

Copernicus turned this theory on its
head by radically contending that the
sun was at the center of the universe,
and that the Earth spun once daily on
its axis and revolved yearly around the sun. His theory was known
as the heliocentric or sun-centered theory of the universe.

Copernicus's paper was not published until 1543, just prior to his death.
At the time, not many scientists believed in his theory, Galileo and the
German astronomer Johannes Kelper being two of the few supporters.

It was not until the work of Sir Isaac
Newton in the late seventeenth century
that astronomers began to accept
Copernicus's Theory.

114 FAST FACT...

📖 **IN 1588**, British mathematician
William Bourne designed a
submarine. It was made of wood
and waterproofed leather and was
rowed like a boat.

115 FAST FACT...

📖 **IVAN THE TERRIBLE** (1547–1584) beat his own son to death in a fit of rage.

116 FAST FACT...

📖 **"TO GOD** I speak Spanish, to women Italian, to men French, and to my horse - German."
– Emperor Charles V (1500–1558)

117 1547 IVAN THE TERRIBLE BECOMES FIRST TSAR OF RUSSIA

IVAN VI VASILYVICH was crowned the first Tsar of all Russia in 1547. He would later earn the nickname "Ivan the Terrible" for his cruel, ruthless and often brutal style of leadership. He famously killed his own son during a furious argument.

His monarchy saw the introduction of many reforms: the law code was revised, a standing army created, and the Church unified. Ivan introduced the system of serfdom and ordered the building of St Basil's Cathedral in Moscow (he then blinded the architects to prevent them from building anything as magnificent again).

Ivan led successful campaigns against the Tatar strongholds of Kazan, Astrakhan and, after expanding into Siberia, transformed Russia into a multi-ethnic and multi-religious state.

After the death of his wife, Anastasia, in 1560, Ivan became increasingly violent and paranoid, creating an elite police force (the Oprichniki) to hunt down suspected traitors. Many noblemen had their lands confiscated and were tortured or executed. In 1570, the entire city of Novgorod was massacred after Ivan suspected its citizens of committing treason.

When Ivan the Terrible died in 1582 Russia, in the midst of military defeats, economic setbacks and famine, was left ravaged.

St Basil's Cathedral, Moscow

118 FAST FACT...
IVAN THE TERRIBLE was killed while playing chess.

119 FAST FACT...
LADY JANE GREY was Queen of England for just nine days before being beheaded in 1554.

120 FAST FACT...
FRENCH VISIONARY Nostradamus is said to have predicted the Great Fire of London, the French Revolution and both World Wars – all in 1555.

121 FAST FACT...
THE WORST EARTHQUAKE in history occurred in Shansi Province, China, in 1556. It killed around 830,000 people.

122 1600 FOUNDING OF THE EAST INDIA COMPANY

🎓 **THE DEFEAT** of the Spanish Armada in 1588 opened up the possibility of British involvement in the spice trade, which had previously been controlled by the Spanish and Portuguese.

123 FAST FACT...

📖 **EMPEROR AKBAR** of India was so impressed with the Persian tutor of his three sons that each year he paid him their combined weight in gold.

The East India Company (or Governor and Company of Merchants of London Trading into the East Indies) was a shared-stock company of wealthy London merchants seeking to profit from the import of spices from South Asia. It was founded on December 31, 1600, when Elizabeth I of England signed a Royal Charter granting the company a 15-year monopoly on all trade in the East Indies. It went on to trade for almost 200 years.

The Company established trading posts and factories in Bantam, Surat, Bombay (now Mumbai) and Calcutta (now Kolkata), and fought off opposition from other traders such as the Dutch and Portuguese (defeating the latter in the Battle of Swally in 1612). Trading in tea, salt, pepper, indigo dye, silk, cotton, saltpetre, and opium, the Company expanded into the Persian Gulf and Southeast Asia.

The Company ruled huge swathes of India, which it controlled using its own military. It was dissolved in 1874 when the East India Stock Dividend Redemption Act was introduced.

124 FAST FACT...

📖 **SIR WALTER RALEIGH** (1522–1618) was smoking a pipe one day when a servant threw a bucket of water over him, thinking he was on fire – he hadn't yet heard of tobacco.

125 FAST FACT...

📖 **IN 1582**, Pope Gregory XIII decreed that 10 days should be skipped as the Julian calendar in use at the time was 11 minutes too long. There were riots, as people thought their lives had been shortened.

126 FAST FACT...

📖 **THE 1591 WAR** between Burma and Thailand was decided by single combat between the two princes, each riding an elephant. The Burmese prince was killed.

127 1603 JAMES VI CROWNED JAMES I OF ENGLAND

AFTER THE FORCED abdication of Mary Queen of Scots in 1567, Prince James was crowned King James VI of Scotland at the age of 13 months. When his mother's cousin, Queen Elizabeth I of England, died in 1603, he was crowned James I of England, becoming the first monarch to rule both Scotland and England.

King James was one of England's most learned and controversial monarchs; his reign was dogged by rumors of his alleged homosexuality. He nevertheless fathered three surviving children by his wife, Anne of Denmark. He was an unpopular ruler who caused conflicts within Parliament with his foreign policy of improving England's relationship with Spain, and he alienated both Puritans and Catholics by asserting the supreme authority and divine right of the crown. He gained temporary popularity when he thwarted an attempt by Guy Fawkes to blow up the Houses of Parliament.

He was an avid supporter of literature and the arts and was responsible for ordering the printing of the King James Bible of 1611, which remains the most printed book in history.

King James died of senility in 1625 and is buried at Westminster Abbey.

128 FAST FACT...

IN 1604, a monk named Gregory Otrepiev claimed he was the heir to the Russian throne. Amazingly, people believed him and Otrepiev became Tsar.

Vintage engraving from 1878 showing female pirates.

129 FAST FACT...

TWO OF THE MOST notorious pirates of the seventeenth century were women – Ann Bonny and Mary Read.

KINGS AND QUEENS OF ENGLAND SINCE 1066

NAME AND DYNASTY	ACCESSION	DEATH
HOUSE OF NORMANDY		
William I	1066	1087
William II	1087	1100
Henry I	1100	1135
Stephen	1135	1154
HOUSE OF PLANTAGENET		
Henry II	1154	1189
Richard I *(Richard Coeur de Lion)*	1189	1199
John	1199	1216
Henry III	1216	1272
Edward I	1272	1307
Edward II	1307	1327
Edward III	1327	1377
Richard II	1377	1399 *(deposed)*
HOUSE OF LANCASTER		
Henry IV	1399	1413
Henry V	1413	1422
Henry VI	1422	1461 *(deposed)*
HOUSE OF YORK		
Edward IV	1461	1483
Edward V	1483	1483
Richard III	1483	1485
HOUSE OF TUDOR		
Henry VII	1485	1509
Henry VIII	1509	1547
Edward VI	1547	1553
Jane Grey	1553	1553
Mary I	1553	1558
Elizabeth I	1558	1603

NAME AND DYNASTY	ACCESSION	DEATH
HOUSE OF STUART		
James I *(VI of Scotland)*	1603	1625
Charles I	1625	1649 *(beheaded)*
COMMONWEALTH DECLARED 1649		
Oliver Cromwell, Lord Protector	1653–58	
Richard Cromwell, Lord Protector	1658–59	
Charles II	1660 *(restored)*	1685
James II (VII of Scotland)	1685	1688 *(deposed)*, 1701 *(died)*
William III and Mary II	1689	1702
Anne	1702	1714
HOUSE OF HANOVER		
George I	1714	1727
George II	1727	1760
George III	1760	1820
George IV	1820	1830
William IV	1830	1837
Victoria	1837	1901
HOUSE OF SAXE-COBURG		
Edward VII	1901	1910
HOUSE OF SAXE-COBURG (HOUSE OF WINDSOR FROM 1917)		
George V	1910	1936
Edward VIII	1936	1936 *(abdicated)*
George VI	1936	1952
Elizabeth II	1952	–

130 1605 THE GUNPOWDER PLOT

🎓 **WHEN PROTESTANT** King James VI of Scotland was crowned James I of England, English Catholics hoped he would be tolerant of their religion. They were disappointed and angered when he continued to impose restrictions, fines and various other punishments upon Catholics who refused to attend Anglican Church services. In February 1604 he ordered all Catholic priests to leave the country, and in April the same year introduced a bill in Parliament that was to persecute all followers of the Catholic faith.

As a consequence, a group of 13 conspirators, led by Robert Catesby, devised a plot to kill King James and blow up the Houses of Parliament. If their plan succeeded, the conspirators hoped to install King James's daughter, Elizabeth, on the throne as Catholic head of state.

Thirty-six barrels of gunpowder were stored in a cellar under parliament, and one of the men, Guy Fawkes, was chosen to ignite the explosives on November 5, when Parliament opened and the King would be in attendance.

The plot was foiled when one of the conspirators sent an anonymous letter to Lord Monteagle warning him to stay away from Parliament. The cellars were searched and Guy Fawkes was caught and executed for treason.

To this day in England, every November 5 is commemorated by fireworks and the burning of a "guy" on a bonfire.

Words, words words...and more words!

131 FAST FACT...

📖 **WILLIAM SHAKESPEARE** (c. 1564–1616) used about 29,000 words in his plays, 10,000 of which had never been used before in any written work.

132 FAST FACT...

📖 **IN 1613**, London's Globe Theatre burned down when a spark from a stage cannon set fire to the roof during a performance of *Henry VIII*.

133 1606 DUTCH DISCOVER AUSTRALIA

DUTCH NAVIGATOR Willem Janszoon was employed by the Dutch East India Company, after having first traveled from the Netherlands to the Dutch East Indies in 1598.

In 1605 he was instructed by the president of the East India Company to captain an expedition to explore the coast of New Guinea, in the hope of discovering gold or new sources of profitable trading opportunities.

134 FAST FACT...

IN 17th-century Europe, *"corpse medicine"* – medicine made from parts of dead bodies – was very popular.

His vessel, the *Duyfken*, set sail from Bantam in west Java in September 1605 with a crew of 20. After exploring the New Guinea coastline, Janszoon sailed south across the Arafura Sea – completely missing the Torres Strait – and into the Gulf of Carpentaria. In February 1606 he landed on the western shore of Cape York Peninsula in Queensland and became the first known European to set foot in Australia.

Still believing the land to be part of New Guinea, he continued to chart the coastline until violent encounters with the Aborigines at Cape Keerweer (Dutch for Cape Turnabout) forced him into retreat.

135 FAST FACT...

TULIPS became extremely popular in 17th-century Holland. One sailor was thrown in prison for eating a tulip bulb – he thought it was an onion.

136 1607 ENGLISH COLONY OF JAMESTOWN FOUNDED

IN 1605, two English merchant groups combined to form the Virginia Company and raised the capital needed to establish an American colony.

On May 14, 1607, around 200 English colonists landed at Chesapeake Bay, North America and founded Jamestown, Virginia – named after King James I of England. The site chosen proved at first to be a disastrous choice, when famine, drought, disease and continual attacks from the local tribes killed all but 60 of the original settlers.

Captain John Smith assumed leadership and began to earn the trust of Chief Powhatan of the Algonquian tribe. It was only through the help of the Algonquians – who gave food in exchange for tools and beads – that any of the settlers survived the first harsh winter.

Hostilities broke out once more when the colonists began to expand their territory, and a temporary peace was only reached when colonist John Rolfe married Pocahontas, the daughter of Chief Powhatan.

Captain John Smith (1580–1631)

Rolfe was instrumental in the turnaround of Jamestown's fortunes, turning tobacco into a lucrative export and attracting more settlers.

By 1619 the parliamentary House of Burgess had been formed and North America was on its way to having its first democratic government.

An engraving from 1874
showing the construction
of the Jamestown settlement

137 1618 THIRTY YEARS WAR BEGINS

THE THIRTY YEARS WAR began as a religious conflict, fought between the Protestants and Catholics of Germany. It went on to draw in most of the major European powers and became increasingly complicated when other issues such as political power struggles, territorial disputes, and commercial control became involved.

The inciting incident, which came to be known as the Defenestration of Prague, took place on May 23, 1618, when an angry mob of Bohemian Protestant nobles invaded the Hradschin Castle in Prague and threw three representatives of the devout Catholic (and soon to be new emperor) Archduke Ferdinand II of Austria, out of a window.

The war was divided into four distinct periods: The Bohemian Revolt, the Danish Intervention, the Swedish Intervention and the French Intervention. Around 40 separate battles were fought, including the Battle of White Mountain (1620), the Battle of Breitenfeld (1631), and the Battle of Nordlingen (1634).

The Thirty Years War was one of the most destructive wars in European history and saw the German population almost halved.

Sir Walter Raleigh
(1552-1618)

138 FAST FACT...

FOLLOWING his execution in 1618, Sir Walter Raleigh's wife kept his embalmed head in a bag for 29 years.

139 1620 THE VOYAGE OF THE PILGRIM FATHERS

ON SEPTEMBER 15, 1620, the Pilgrim Fathers, a group of English Puritans who had separated themselves from the Anglican Church, set sail from the port of Plymouth, England, aboard the *Mayflower* to create a new settlement in Colonial America that would be free from religious persecution.

140 FAST FACT...

📖 **ENGLISH PHILOSOPHER**
Francis Bacon invented frozen food by stuffing a chicken with snow in 1625. He died of pneumonia soon afterwards.

Captained by Christopher Jones, the ship headed for the mouth of the Hudson River, near Virginia, but rough seas pushed it off-course and forced a landing at Cape Cod Bay in early November. At this point, some 50 non-Puritan passengers declared themselves exempt from English rule. Unable to allow any form of dissent at this early stage, the Pilgrim leaders drew up the Mayflower Compact, a set of laws by which all men on board agreed to abide, and elected John Carver as governor of the colony.

The *Mayflower* set sail again and landed at Plymouth Rock in late December, where the Pilgrim Fathers began to build the first settlement house. Disease and the harsh winter killed almost half of the colonists. With the help of the Wampanoag tribe of Native Americans, the rest of the colony survived and the first harvest was celebrated with a feast of turkey, pumpkins and corn.

The Mayflower, the ship that transported the first European settlers to North America.

141 FAST FACT...

📖 **IN 1649**, the New World colony of Massachussetts declared that the punishment for stubbornness was death.

142 1641 THE MERCHANT ROYAL SHIPWRECK

🎓 **THE MERCHANT ROYAL** was a 700-ton merchant ship, built in London in 1627. Captained by John Limbrey, the ship spent from 1637–1640 trading with the Spanish colonies.

After landing at Cadiz, in southern Spain, the *Merchant Royal* began to leak and had to undergo extensive repairs. At around the same time, a Spanish ship, due to set sail from Cadiz with a cargo of Spanish bullion (wages for Spain's 30,000-strong army stationed in Flanders), caught fire. Seeing a chance to profit from the disaster, Captain Limbrey volunteered to transport the bullion to Antwerp on his voyage back to England.

143 FAST FACT...

📖 **BETWEEN** 1500 and 1650, Spanish conquistadors shipped 198 tons of gold from the Americas back to Europe.

The *Merchant Royal*, accompanied by her sister ship the *Dover Merchant*, set sail from Cadiz in August 1641. The recent repairs did not hold and the ship began to leak badly, eventually capsizing off Land's End, Cornwall on September 23, 1641. Eighteen crew members drowned and the rest were rescued by the *Dover Merchant*.

The bullion lost amounted to several tons of silver, and gold coins and ingots, and made the *Merchant Royal* the most valuable shipwreck of all time.

THE ENGLISH CIVIL WAR began in 1642 under the reign of Charles I.

King Charles believed in the Divine Right of Kings and refused to let Parliament influence issues such as taxes and religion. In 1629, he locked the doors of Westminster, preventing members of parliament from meeting. This period was called the Eleven Years Tyranny, or Charles's Personal Rule.

The split between King and Parliament grew, and when the king raised an army to quell a rebellion against English rule in Ireland, Parliament feared the army would be used against them. Under the leadership of John Pym, the Grand Remonstrance was adopted, which demanded parliamentary control over the army, Church reform and royal appointments. Charles I responded by having Pym arrested and civil war became inevitable. Charles raised his standard at Nottingham on August 22, 1641.

There were three major battles of the Civil War: Edge Hill (1642), Marston Moor (1644) and Naseby (1645), which saw Royalist supporters (Cavaliers) pitted against Parliamentarians (Roundheads) and Oliver Cromwell's New Model Army.

In 1646, Charles I surrendered to the Scots and was tried for treason on January 1, 1649. He was beheaded on January 30, 1649. A Council of State was set up and for 11 years – for the only time in its history – England was without a monarch.

An engraving from 1846 showing a scene from the English Civil War (1642–1651)

145 1644 THE MANCHUS UNITE AND CONQUER MING EMPIRE

THE MANCHUS originated from northeast of the Great Wall of China. A tribal people, they were skilled archers and horsemen and had been forcibly united in around 1607 by the Tungu Prince Nurhaci, the founder of the Manchurian state.

The Ming Dynasty, under the rule of the last Ming emperor, Chongzhen, had begun to decline in around 1628. Threats from barbarian invaders, peasant revolts, poor harvests, political in-fighting and a moral decline within the army had all taken their toll.

In 1644, a former Ming official, Li Zicheng, led a peasant revolt that defeated Ming armies in the Sichuan and Henan Provinces, and invaded Beijing. The weakened city fell easily and Ming Emperor Chongzhen committed suicide. With no opposition left, Li Zicheng declared himself emperor of the new Shun Dynasty. It was to be a short-lived reign.

Within a day, the Shun Dynasty was overthrown. In the wake of the peasant revolt, Ming general, Wu Sangui, had allied with the Manchus and opened the Shanghai Pass to the Manchurian army. Beijing was seized and Hong Taiji, Khan of Manchuria, became Emperor Tiancong of China, establishing the Qing Dynasty.

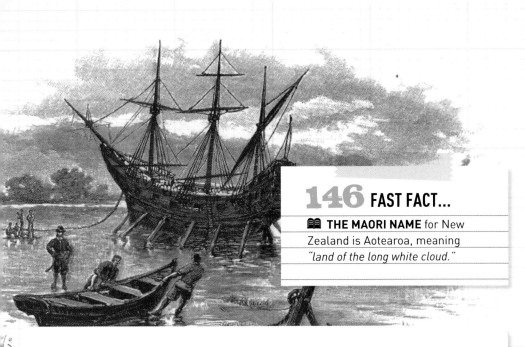

146 FAST FACT...

📖 **THE MAORI NAME** for New Zealand is Aotearoa, meaning *"land of the long white cloud."*

147 1768 JAMES COOK DISCOVERS NEW ZEALAND

JAMES COOK was born in Yorkshire, England in 1728. He trained as a seaman and also studied algebra, astronomy, navigation, geometry, and trigonometry. He joined the Royal Navy in 1755, and in 1766 he was promoted to first lieutenant and was given command of the vessel *HMS Bark Endeavour*.

His first expedition as commander saw him sail from Plymouth on August 26, 1768 across the Pacific Ocean to Tahiti to observe and record the transit of Venus across the sun. In addition, he was instructed by the Admiralty to search for signs of the supposed southern continent, Terra Australis.

After four months in Tahiti, the *Endeavour* set sail to the south into what were then unchartered waters. On October 6, 1769, cabin boy Nicolas Young sighted land and the *Endeavour* anchored at what Cook would name Poverty Bay in New Zealand. The crew's first encounter with the native Maori ended in hostility and Cook continued to sail the *Endeavour* south to Cape Turnagain, then north to Tolaga Bay and Anaura Bay.

When Cook finally left New Zealand on March 31, 1770, he had succeeded in mapping 2,400 miles of its coastline.

CHARLES I

BOSTON
TEA PARTY

GOLD

LOUIS XIV

LOUISIANA

SALEM

OLIVER
CROMWELL

VOLTAIRE

VERSAILLES

→ Age of
Reason

BASTILLE

MOZART

CAPE TOWN

AUSTRIA

QUEBEC

FIRE!

148 1648 PEACE OF WESTPHALIA

🎓 **AFTER FIVE YEARS** of negotiations, the Thirty Years War was finally brought to an end on October 28, 1648 with the signing of a series of treaties, specifically the treaties of Munster and Osnabruck, known as the Peace of Westphalia.

Signed between the Holy Roman Emperor (Ferdinand III of the House of Habsburg), Spain, Sweden, France, the Dutch Republic and all their respective allies, the treaties marked the birth of a modern Europe, based on the concept of a sovereign state.

Among the most important of the 128 articles of the treaty were those that gave the Protestant faith of Lutheranism the same status as Catholicism, and officially recognized the religious movement of Calvinism. These motions promoted a measure of religious tolerance, with worshippers being permitted to practice their chosen faith during allotted hours in public, and whenever they wished in private, effectively ending religious warfare in Europe.

There were many territorial adjustments; the Netherlands and Switzerland gained independence, and France gained control of the bishoprics of Metz, Toul, Verdun, Breisach and Philippsburg, and Alsace.

149 FAST FACT...

📖 **ON THE MORNING** of his execution in January 1649, King Charles I wore two shirts. It was cold and he didn't want anyone to think he was shivering with fear.

Charles I (1600–1649)

RIGHT: The trial of King Charles I at Westminster

150 1652 CAPE TOWN FOUNDED

🎓 **EUROPEAN MARITIME TRADERS** on their way to and from the East, had been landing at Table Bay, South Africa since the early sixteenth century in order to replenish their fresh water supplies. It was not until 1647, when the survivors of a Dutch shipwreck at Table Bay reported that the place was hospitable and the natives biddable, that any thought was given to establishing a colony.

Jan Van Riebeeck had joined the Dutch East India Company (the VOC) in 1639. In 1651, he was instructed to sail to the Cape of Good Hope with the aim of establishing an outpost for Dutch trading ships to put in for supplies.

Table Bay, South Africa

Van Riebeeck arrived at the Cape on April 6, 1652 with three ships, around 90 men, and instructions to build a fort and erect a flagpole for signalling to passing ships.

By 1659, Fort Duijnhoop was well established. With its fruit and vegetable gardens and a bartering system with the local Khoikhoi for meat, the small outpost was able to supply any passing ship.

It was not until the VOC granted some of its employees permission to settle and build farms that the outpost (later named Cape Town) became the first European colony in South Africa.

151 FAST FACT...

📖 **ON MARCH 26,** 1658, London diarist Samuel Pepys had a bladder stone the size of a tennis ball removed without an anesthetic.

152 1660 RESTORATION OF THE ENGLISH MONARCHY

BORN ON MAY 29, 1630, Charles II was the eldest surviving son of Charles I, and heir to the English throne. After the English Civil War began in 1642, he was exiled abroad. He was in The Hague, the Netherlands when he learned of his father's execution in 1649.

In 1650, Charles struck a deal with the Scots to lead a Presbyterian invasion of England. He was defeated by Oliver Cromwell (Lord Protector of England, Scotland and Ireland) at the Battle of Worcester on September 3, 1651 and went into exile once more.

When Oliver Cromwell died in 1658, England was divided into two opposing camps: supporters of Cromwell's policies and Royalists who wished to restore the monarchy.

When General Monck (commander of the Protectorate's army in Scotland) realised that Cromwell's son, Richard, would be an incapable successor, he became, along with Edward Hyde, 1st Earl of Clarendon, a leading figure in the move to restore Charles II to the throne.

Monck had the support of his loyal army behind him and Hyde negotiated the Restoration Settlement and the signing of the Declaration of Breda in April 1660, by which Charles II agreed to work with Parliament.

153 FAST FACT...

ONE OF THE FIRST mentions of ice cream in Western Europe came in 1672 when it was served to King Charles II.

154 FAST FACT...

"My words are my own, and my actions are my ministers'." – Charles II (1630–1685)

Charles II (1630–1685)

155 1661 LOUIS XIV RULES AS ABSOLUTE MONARCH

LOUIS XIV, the "Sun King", was born in 1638 in St Germain-en-Laye, France. When his father, Louis XIII, died in 1642, Louis became king at the age of four.

France's monarchy had long relied heavily on the power of cardinal ministers to rule the land. As such, during Louis' childhood his mother, Anne of Austria, served as regent with the assistance of chief minister, Cardinal Mazarin.

156 FAST FACT...

IN 1665, the Great Plague broke out in London, killing around 80,000 people.

When Louis turned 23, Mazarin died and Louis shocked his court by announcing his intention to rule without a chief minister, thereby establishing himself as absolute monarch. After a three-year trial that saw the corrupt finance minister, Nicolas Fouquet, imprisoned for life, the king would go on to control his own government during a reign that lasted for 72 years.

He established a high-state council and selected his own ministers – he did not include family or members of the old nobility. In 1682 he moved his government from Paris to the newly built palace at Versailles.

During his reign he led the 1667–1668 War of Dutch Devolution, when French forces invaded the Habsburg-controlled Netherlands, and in 1685 he controversially revoked the Edict of Nantes, which had given freedom of worship to French Protestants.

Louis XIV's magnificent palace at Versailles.

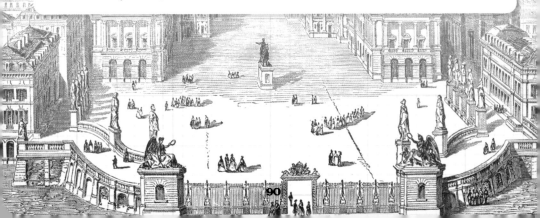

During Louis XIV's reign, France became the leading European power.

157 1666 THE GREAT FIRE OF LONDON

THE GREAT FIRE of London started in Pudding Lane, London, in a bakery owned by Thomas Farynor, baker to King Charles II. On the night of September 2, 1666, a servant woke the household and alerted Farynor and his family to the flames. All but one servant managed to escape.

158 FAST FACT...

THE FIRST successful blood transfusion took place in 1667, when the blood of a sheep was transfused into a teenage boy.

159 FAST FACT...

TSAR PETER the Great (1672–1725) was over 6 feet 6 inches tall.

160 FAST FACT...

THE WORLD'S oldest public museum, the Ashmolean in Oxford, England, opened its doors in 1683.

The weather had been hot and dry all summer and that night, with a strong wind blowing, it did not take long for the fire to spread through the narrow streets, catching the timber-framed houses alight. Within two hours the fire was so well established that it could be seen from over half a mile away.

The mayor of London, Sir Thomas Bloodworth, was instructed by the king to destroy houses in the fire's path in order to create a fire-break. This proved a difficult task due to the speed of the spreading fire, the strength of the wind and the close proximity of the buildings.

It took three days for the fire to eventually die, by which time it had destroyed almost 400 acres of the city, including St Paul's Cathedral, 84 churches and 13,000 homes. It also cleared the city of rats, bringing an end to the plague of 1665.

Vintage engraving of London, England, before the Great Fire.

161 1679 HABEAS CORPUS ACT

🎓 **PASSED IN THE HOUSE OF LORDS** in May 1679, during the reign of King Charles II, the Habeas Corpus Act allowed for an individual to have a fair trial and be given a set sentence.

162 FAST FACT...

📖 **IN 1685,** due to a shortage of coins, the North American colony of New France used playing cards as currency.

Before the act was passed, it was not uncommon for an accused person – especially a political prisoner – to be imprisoned for an undesignated amount of time without his case being examined. This was certainly the case in France at the time. Under the rule of Louis XIV and his *"lettres de cachet,"* anyone who fell under the king's suspicions could be incarcerated indefinitely without legal address.

Translated from the Latin for "You have the body," the Habeas Corpus Act was introduced to the House of Lords by the Earl of Shaftesbury, a leading Exclusionist.

Habeas Corpus was first mentioned in the Magna Carta of 1215; a "writ of Habeas Corpus" could be issued to force someone to appear in court and testify. The 1679 act, however, was understood more as a civil right that protected an individual from being arrested without charge.

163 FAST FACT...

📖 **IN 1686,** Paskah Rose, the newly appointed executioner to King James II of England, was himself hanged for stealing a coat.

Although amended, the statute remains one of the most important in British legal history.

164 1689 THE TREATY OF NERCHINSK

DURING THE 1640'S, at the same time as the Manchus were conquering China, Russia began to expand eastward in a quest for territorial gain and fur trade opportunities.

Between 1652 and 1689 the Russian-Manchu conflicts saw the Russian Cossacks repeatedly repelled by the Manchus in their bid to claim land in the Amur Basin. The hostilities reached their peak in 1686, with the Manchu siege of the Russian fort of Albazin on the Amur River.

Russia appointed Fyodor Golovin as an ambassador to China in a bid to instigate talks with the Qing Dynasty, hoping to iron out border disagreements and to secure trade rights in the Amur valley.

In September 1689, after two weeks of negotiations, the Treaty of Nerchinsk was signed. It was the first modern treaty to be signed by China and a European country and it paved the way for peaceful Sino-Russian relations for the next 165 years. In return for giving up the rights to the Amur valley, the Chinese allowed Russia to keep Nerchinsk as a profitable border trading post.

The Nerchinsk trading post

165 1689 WILLIAM III BECOMES KING OF ENGLAND

🎓 **BORN ON NOVEMBER 4, 1650**

in The Hague, the son of William II of Orange and Mary, daughter of Charles I of England, William became "Stadtholder-King William II (of Orange)" of the Netherlands in 1672.

As military commander and staunch Protestant, William overcame France's invasion of the Netherlands, under Catholic Louis XIV of France, during the Third Anglo-Dutch War, and came to be regarded as a defender of the Protestant faith in Europe.

166 FAST FACT...

📖 **EDWARD TEACH**
(1680–1718), better known as the pirate Blackbeard, would leap into action with exploding firecrackers in his beard.

In 1677, in order to create an Anglo-Dutch alliance against the French, William married his cousin, Mary Stuart, daughter of the Catholic King James II of England. When James produced a male heir to the throne, many of his Protestant opponents, fearing a continuation of Catholic rule, invited William to take the crown, promising him English support.

On November 5, 1688, William landed at Torbay in Devon with over 400 ships and an army of 14,000 soldiers. He advanced unopposed to London and, in what became known as the "Glorious Revolution," he deposed James II.

In February 1689, William and Mary were jointly crowned King William III and Queen Mary II of England.

167 FAST FACT...

📖 **BLACKBEARD** met his end when he leapt aboard a British navy vessel. It took 5 gunshot wounds and 20 sword wounds to kill him.

🗨 A BELIEF IN THE PRACTICE

of witchcraft was widespread from the fourteenth to the seventeenth centuries. Natural disasters, crop failure and illnesses were all believed to be the work of the Devil by many practicing Christians. As a consequence, thousands of suspected witches were tried and executed all across Europe.

This practice had all but died out when unexplained events began to occur in the village of Salem, Massachusetts.

In January 1692, Elizabeth, the nine-year-old daughter of the village's first ordained minister, Reverend Parris, and his eleven-year-old niece, Abigail Williams, both began to behave oddly. Their fits and garbled speech were declared by the local physician to be of supernatural origin. When another girl, eleven-year-old Anne Putnam, began to behave in the same manner, all three were interrogated.

14 women and 5 men were hanged after being found guilty of witchcraft

On February 29, in front of a magistrate, the girls placed the blame for their behavior on three women from the village: Sarah Good, Sarah Osborne and the Parris' Caribbean slave, Tituba. Accused of witchcraft, the women were arrested and imprisoned.

This unleashed a stream of accusations and paranoia, which in the course of a year resulted in the arrests of 200 people and the hanging of 19 of them.

169 1693 GOLD DISCOVERED AT MINAS GERAIS

THE PORTUGUESE bandeirantes were members of South American expeditions which from 1580–1670 hunted and captured Native Americans to be sold into slavery. From 1670 to the mid-eighteenth century, they concentrated instead on finding mineral wealth such as gold, silver and diamonds.

The bandeirantes first discovered large deposits of gold in the unmapped mountains of Minas Gerais (a region in the south-east of Brazil) in 1693, and initiated the Brazil gold rush, leading to the establishment of the city of Ouro Preto (from the Portuguese, Black Gold). The first nuggets of gold found came from the nearby Tripui River and were covered in black iron oxide, thus giving the city its name.

Because of the vast quantities of gold found, Ouro Preto became the wealthiest and most powerful city in Brazil, and was soon established as the capital of Minas Gervais.

170 FAST FACT...

📖 During the "gin craze" of the early 1700's, there were more than 7500 gin shops in London.

Over 400,000 Portuguese and half a million slaves rushed to Minas Gervais to mine the gold and many sugar plantations on the northeast coast were abandoned by the promise of greater riches. Wanting to hold on to its wealth, Ouro Preto attempted a rebellion against Portugal. It was an unmitigated failure and when the gold mines became depleted, Ouro Preto fell into obscurity.

171 FAST FACT...

📖 **SIR ISAAC NEWTON'S** only recorded speech as a Member of Parliament was a request to open the window.

172 1699 FRENCH COLONY OF LOUISIANA FOUNDED

IN 1682, French explorer René-Robert Cavelier, Sieur de La Salle, was commissioned by King Louis XIV to lead an expedition to sail the length of the Mississippi River in order to explore, map and establish fur trade routes. He named the entire region Louisiana, in honor of the King. But as a settlement was not yet established, the French claim to the area was not viable.

It was not until the late 1690's that moves to colonize Louisiana were initiated. Pierre Le Moyne d'Iberville, trader, explorer and ship captain, was tasked with leading an expedition to rediscover the mouth of the Mississippi, and to establish a colony before the English got there. In October 1698, Iberville and a fleet of ships sailed from Brest to the Gulf Coast, arriving in January 1699.

Iberville gained the trust of the local Biloxi natives by plying them with gifts. From them he learned the location of the Mississippi. Unable to find a suitable location along the river to build a fort, Iberville returned to the eastern side of Biloxi Bay and in April 1699, constructed the fort (named Maurepas), and founded the capital of the French colony of Louisiana that was to become known as Baton Rouge.

173 FAST FACT...

In the eighteenth century, executioners earned extra money by cutting the heads off their victims and then selling them for medical investigation.

A group of men counting money on top of a grave, in eighteenth-century England.

174 FAST FACT...

DURING the eighteenth century, anatomists often paid grave robbers to steal newly buried bodies so they could dissect them.

🎓 **THE BATTLE OF BLENHEIM** was a decisive battle that took place during the War of Spanish Succession (1701–1714).

In 1700, when Charles II of Spain died leaving no heir, both King Louis XIV of France and Emperor Leopold I of Austria (Habsburg Empire), made claims to the Spanish throne and Spain's territory. War was declared and soon spread across Europe.

In 1701, the Grand Alliance was formed between England, the Dutch Republic, Portugal, Spain, and the Habsburg Empire. In 1704, Louis XIV, in alliance with Bavaria, made moves to capture Vienna (the capital of the Habsburg Empire) and gain a suitable peace settlement.

Anxious to avoid the invasion and to keep the Grand Alliance intact, the Duke of Marlborough (commander of the English and Dutch forces) made plans to intercept the Franco-Bavarian army en route to Vienna. Using a combination of deception and tactical brilliance, Marlborough succeeded in marching his army some 250 miles from the Low Countries to the River Danube, where on August 13, 1704 he defeated the French and Bavarians and ensured the safety of Vienna.

176 1707 DEATH OF MUGHAL EMPEROR AURANGZEB

🎓 **BORN NOVEMBER 4, 1618,** Aurangzeb was nine years old when his father (Shah Jahan) became emperor of the Mughal Empire, India.

As a young man, Aurangzeb was appointed Governor of Gujarat and helped to extend the already vast Moghul Empire northwards and southwards.

In 1657, when the emperor became ill, Aurangzeb and his three brothers began to fight for the throne. Aurangezeb made a pact with one brother, Murad, promising him the throne if together they defeated the other two brothers.

The emperor partially recovered his health, but by this time the fight for the throne had gone too far. Aurangezeb arranged for the execution of his three brothers, including his former ally Murad, and had his father placed under house arrest before seizing the throne for himself.

Aurangezeb was to rule for 48 years, but as an intolerant and orthodox emperor, his reign was beset with problems. His constant warring stretched the empire's resources and his religious intolerance roused opposition from the Marathas and the Sikhs.

When Aurangezeb died on February 20, 1707, he left the declining Empire in a weakened condition. It never fully recovered and by 1858, the British had moved into India and established the British Raj.

177 FAST FACT...

📖 **IN 1718,** James Puckle invented the first machine gun. The Puckle gun could fire nine shots per minute.

178 1707 ACT OF UNION UNITES SCOTLAND AND ENGLAND

ENGLAND AND SCOTLAND had shared the same monarch since 1603, when King James VI of Scotland was crowned James I of England.

Although there had been attempts to formally unite the two countries, none had proved successful. The first attempt by King James in 1606 was given little consideration by a Parliament concerned that a formal allegiance with Scotland may mean a return to a state of absolute monarchy. During Cromwell's time as Lord Protector of England, he created "An Ordinance by the Protector for the Union of England and Scotland." This was ratified as an Act of Union in 1657, but was immediately dissolved when Charles II was restored to the throne.

By the early eighteenth century, the political needs of both countries to form a union had increased. Scotland required economic security and assistance, while England needed to secure Scottish support against possible French attack.

In 1706 the Parliaments of England and Scotland drew up the Treaty of Union. Consisting of 25 articles, all voted on separately, the treaty was ratified in January 1707 and went into effect on May 1, 1707, heralding the birth of the United Kingdom.

James I (1566-1625) was the first monarch to rule both England and Scotland, but it was not until 1707 that the two countries were formally united.

179 1740 WAR OF AUSTRIAN SUCCESSION

WHEN CHARLES VI, Emperor of Austria, died in October 1740, he left the throne to his daughter, Maria Theresa. The newly crowned King of Prussia, Frederick II, violated the Pragmatic Sanction (under which the great European powers had agreed to accept Maria Theresa as heir to the Habsburg throne) and in December 1740, invaded the historical region of Silesia. This act initiated a series of campaigns that ran from 1740–1748 and were known as the "War of Austrian Succession" or "King George's War."

All of Europe became involved, with France, Spain, Bavaria, and Prussia fighting against Austria's Pragmatic Army and Britain (which had joined the war under George II to guard against a Europe dominated by France).

Three of the greatest battles of the war occurred in the year 1745. The Battles of Hohenfriedberg and Kesselsdorf were both won by the Prussian army. The Battle of Fontenoy, fought between the Pragmatic Allies and France, proved to be one of the most important battles of the whole war, leading to the French conquest of much of the Austrian Netherlands.

The War of Austrian Succession was brought to an end on October 18, 1748 by the signing of the Treaty of Aix-le-Chapelle. All conquered lands, except for Silesia, were restored.

180 FAST FACT...

THE WAR of Jenkins's Ear, fought between England and Spain, erupted in 1739 after the Spanish cut off the ear of Captain Robert Jenkins.

182 FAST FACT...

IN 1740, a French cow was found guilty of sorcery and hanged.

181 FAST FACT...

AFTER "gentleman highwayman" James MacLaine (1724–1750) accidentally shot the writer Horace Walpole during a hold-up, he sent him a letter of apology.

183 FAST FACT...

THE WORLD'S first elevator was installed by Louis XV of France in 1743. He called it his "flying chair".

184 1745 JACOBITE REBELLION

WHEN JAMES II of England was forced to abdicate in 1688, supporters of the Stuart claim to the throne became known as Jacobites (Jacobus being the Latin name for James).

France, as a Catholic nation, had always supported the Stuart claim to the English crown. In 1744, Louis XV offered to fund another attempt to gain the throne back. (Two previous attempts – one in 1690 by James II and another in 1715 by James Francis Stuart – had both failed).

185 FAST FACT...

📖 **BIOLOGICAL WARFARE** began in 1758 when British settlers tried to infect Native Americans by giving them blankets from dead smallpox patients.

Charles Edward Stuart (or Bonnie Prince Charlie), the grandson of James II, was to lead the invasion. Charles set sail for Scotland, landing in the Outer Hebrides in July 1745. Gathering support from the north-east and the Highland clans, he captured Edinburgh and advanced to Derby. But the promised French troops did not arrive and he received little support from the English Catholics. Forced to retreat to Scotland, Charles was pursued by the English army and was finally defeated in the Battle of Culloden in April 1746 (the last major battle to be fought in the United Kingdom), bringing an end to the Jacobite Rebellions and hastening the demise of the Highland clan system.

186 FAST FACT...

📖 **PRECOCIOUS COMPOSER**
Wolfgang Amadeus Mozart (1756–1791) wrote his first compositions aged five.

Wolfgang Amadeus
Mozart (1756–1791)

187 1756–63 SEVEN YEARS WAR

THE SEVEN YEARS WAR was the first global war in history, claiming around 1.5 million casualties. It was fought on two fronts: in Europe between Austria, Prussia and their allies (still nursing grievances following the War of Austrian Succession), and in America between England, France, and Spain (all struggling for colonial supremacy). The war on the American front came to be known as the French-Indian War.

With France allied with Austria, England entered the war on the side of Prussia and, in a series of naval conflicts, managed to break France's hold on its colonies. By 1760, France had relinquished its hold on its American territories and all of North America east of the Mississippi came under British control. The Anglo-French hostilities were brought to an end by the signing of the Treaty of Paris in 1763.

In Europe, Frederick II of Prussia, despite being pitted against the three major powers of Austria, France and Russia, invaded and captured Saxony in October 1756, and by the end of the war (brought about by the signing of the Treaty of Hubertusburg in February 1763) had managed to maintain possession of Silesia. This marked the beginning of the modern German state.

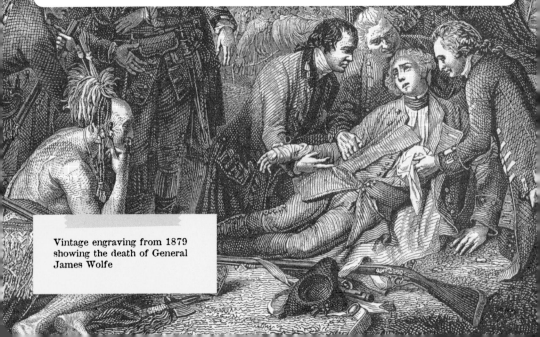

Vintage engraving from 1879 showing the death of General James Wolfe

188 1759 THE BATTLE OF QUEBEC

THE BATTLE OF QUEBEC was one of the battles of the Seven Years War. It took place on September 13, 1759 and was fought between the English army (led by Major-General James Wolfe) and the French army (led by the Marquis de Montcalm).

In August 1758, the British had defeated the French in the Battle of Carillon and taken control of Louisbourg. This victory opened up the sea route to Quebec, and the walled city became the next military target of the British offensive.

In June 1759, General James Wolfe led a fleet of 250 ships carrying around 9000 troops up the St Lawrence River to the city of Quebec. Being protected by high, inaccessible cliffs, the city was able to resist a three-month-long siege. In a bid to force the French into conflict, Wolfe deployed 5000 of his men to land south-west of the city in L'Anse-au-Foulon cove. Under cover of darkness, a small number of men climbed the cliffs and seized control of a minor road. The rest of the troops followed and forced the French into battle on the Plains of Abraham.

A decisive British victory, the short battle saw both Wolfe and Montcalm lose their lives, and the French lose grip on their North American territories.

189 FAST FACT...

GEORGE III became king of England in 1760. He suffered from poor mental health and came to be known as "Mad King George."

190 FAST FACT...

GEORGE III and his wife, Charlotte of Mecklenburg-Strelitz, had 15 children.

191 FAST FACT...

THE TUNE for the American national anthem was composed in 1765 by Englishman John Stafford Smith. The lyrics come from Francis Scott Key's poem "Defence of Fort McHenry" (1814).

192 FAST FACT...

ENGLISH prisoner William Addis was serving time in 1770 when he invented the first mass-produced toothbrush.

193 1763 THE TREATY OF PARIS

SIGNED ON February 10, 1763 by France, Britain and Spain, after three years of negotiations, the Treaty of Paris finally ended the Seven Years War and its American counterpart, the French-Indian War.

Under the terms of the treaty, Britain emerged with a large empire, having gained Canada (including east of the Mississippi River and the Great Lakes Basin), Cape Breton Island, Florida, Grenada, the Grenadines, and Minorca.

France lost most of its territory in North America but retained fishing rights in Newfoundland and had its trading posts in India restored. It also agreed to withdraw its armies from the German states.

Spain realized few of its war aims, regaining Manila and Havana, receiving New Orleans and west Louisiana from France, but having to restore all other captured territory back to its original holders.

Britain's ally, Frederick II of Prussia, was forced to negotiate his own separate peace terms with Russia and Saxony with the signing of the Hubertusburg Treaty on February 15, 1763.

194 FAST FACT...

"Give me liberty or give me death" – American revolutionary Patrick Henry (1736–1799), from a speech given in 1775.

195 FAST FACT...

ON BEING ASKED to renounce the Devil, on his deathbed in 1778, French philosopher Voltaire replied: *"This is no time for making new enemies."*

196 FAST FACT...

THE FIRST parachute jump from an aircraft took place in 1785 when a dog was dropped from a hot-air balloon.

197 FAST FACT...

"I shall be an autocrat: that's my trade. And the good Lord will forgive me: that's his." – Empress Catherine the Great of Russia (1729–1796).

198 1770 THE BOSTON MASSACRE

TENSIONS BETWEEN AMERICAN colonists and the British government had been growing since the introduction of the Townshend Acts of 1767, which were designed to collect revenue from the colonists by taxing imports such as paper, tea and glass. The Acts proved to be very unpopular and colonists reacted angrily when British troops were sent to Boston to keep the peace and enforce the Acts.

On March 5, 1770 a British sentry, Private Hugh White, became involved in a fight with a barber's apprentice. When the brawl attracted a mob of angry colonists, British troops were called to the scene, led by Captain Thomas Preston. In the ensuing confusion, a number of shots were fired into the crowd and three colonists were killed. Two more died later as a result of their wounds.

Captain Preston and eight other British soldiers were arrested and tried for murder. Defended by leading Patriot, John Adams, all but two of the soldiers were acquitted. The convicted soldiers were found guilty of manslaughter and given reduced sentences.

The incident became know as the Boston Massacre. It fuelled anti-British resentment and brought the colonists a step closer to revolution.

199 1773 THE BOSTON TEA PARTY

ON MAY 10, 1773, British Parliament passed the Tea Act, which granted the beleaguered British East India Company a monopoly on tea sales in the American colonies. The Act relieved the company of the burden of paying tax on tea and enabled them to undercut any rival colonial tea merchants.

Although not intended to stir up ill feeling in the American colonies, the Act nonetheless angered the colonists, who saw the move as an underhand attempt by the British government to force them into buying British produce. A boycott of British tea was decreed and when three East India Company ships docked in Boston Harbor in November 1773, angry colonists refused to unload the cargo and demanded the ships returned to England. A standoff ensued when the governor of Massachusetts ordered the harbor to be blockaded until the ships were unloaded.

200 FAST FACT...

THE MUMMIFIED heart of French king Louis XIV was stolen during the French Revolution and may have later been eaten by English geologist William Buckland.

On the night of December 16, 1773, members of the Sons of Liberty, disguised as Native Americans, boarded the ships and tipped 342 chests of tea into the harbor. An outraged British Parliament reacted by passing the Intolerable Acts of 1774, which placed further restrictions on the colonists and moved them to form the first Continental Congress.

201 FAST FACT...

FRENCH FRIES were actually invented in Belgium in the 1790's.

202 1789 THE STORMING OF THE BASTILLE

THE REIGN OF KING LOUIS XVI of France was beset by financial difficulties. Starvation was threatening the population and the need for reforms had become absolutely paramount.

The King summoned the Estates-General (representatives from the Church, the nobility and the common people) to an assembly, in order to find solutions to the financial crisis and discuss the inevitable rise in taxes.

The First and Second Estates (the clergy and nobility) were to meet in separate houses from the Third Estate, ensuring that the common people would always be outvoted. When the Third Estate's demands for all three Estates to sit together were refused, many members peeled away and formed a National Assembly. The first act of the National Assembly was to issue a "Declaration of the Rights of Man."

Members of the First and Second Estates moved to join the National Assembly and when news of a royal counter-attack spread, the people of Paris stormed the ancient prison of Bastille, which had long been a symbol of the corrupt and absolute monarchy. This act signalled the beginning of the French Revolution and changed the way the country was governed forever.

203 FAST FACT...

IN 1786, Frenchwoman Marie-Augustin was sent to prison for 50 years for whistling at Queen Marie-Antoinette as she was entering a theater..

204 FAST FACT...

DURING the French Revolution, Marie Tussaud of waxwork fame made death masks of famous victims of guillotine.

205 FAST FACT...

LOUIS XVI, who was beheaded by the guillotine, actually helped to design it.

206 FAST FACT...

IN 1795, the French chef Nicholas Appert won first prize in a competition to find the best way of preserving food. His suggestion was to use a tin can.

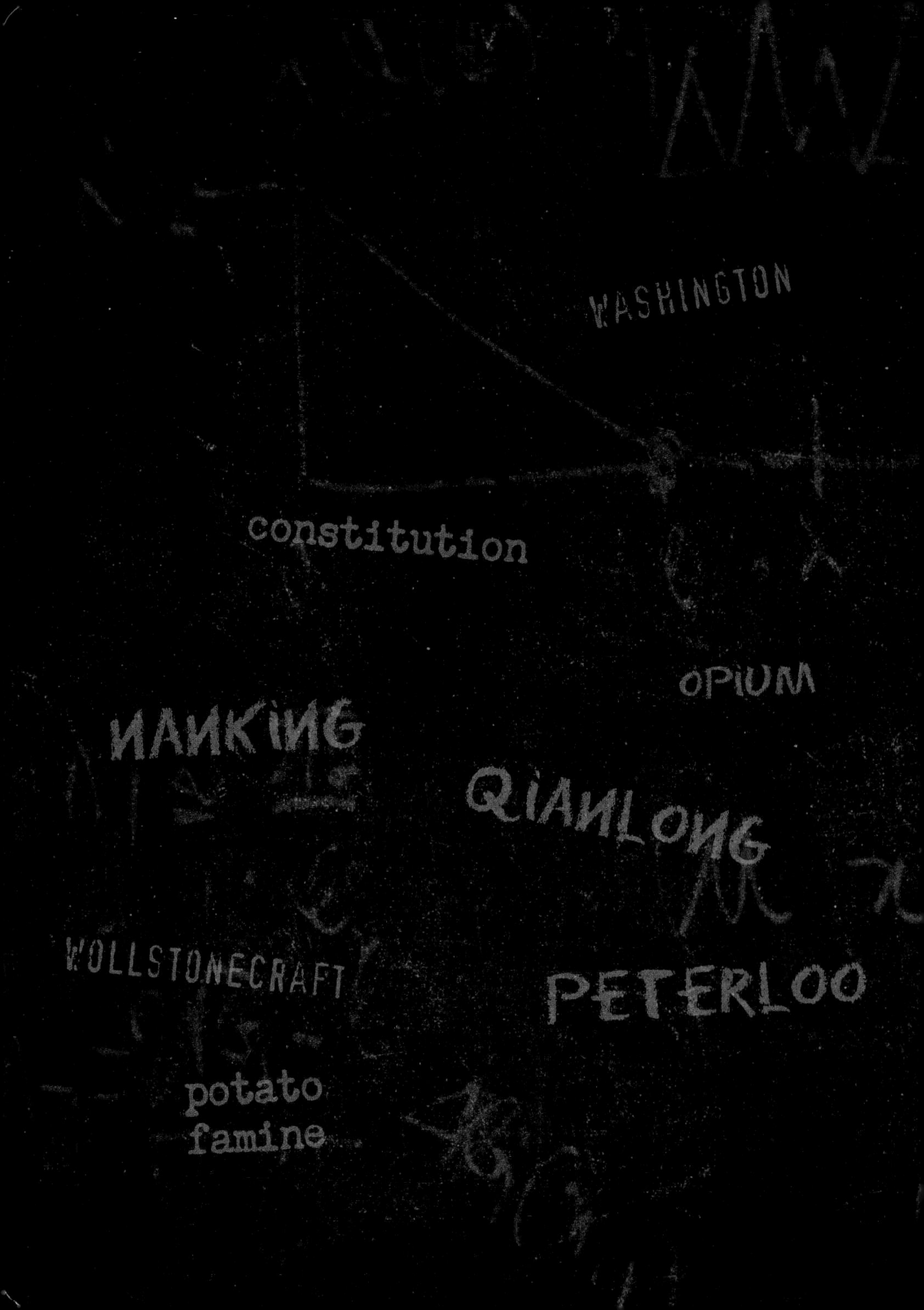

WASHINGTON

constitution

OPIUM

NANKING

QIANLONG

WOLLSTONECRAFT

PETERLOO

potato
famine

INDEPENDENCE

NELSON

Rebellion

ALAMO

NAPOLEON

REFORM

FREEDOM

Adam
Smith

LIBERTY

207 1775–1783 AMERICAN WAR OF INDEPENDENCE

THE AMERICAN WAR of Independence (or the American Revolutionary War) erupted in 1775, when the 13 British colonies in North America became utterly disillusioned with the powers of the British government and the perceived unfairness of the Stamp Act of 1765, the Townshend Acts of 1767 and later the Intolerable Acts of 1774, which were passed by British parliament in the hope of quelling growing colonial disobedience.

While the British had an unrivalled navy and a well-organized army, the Americans relied upon groups of untrained militia men and a strong belief in their cause. The Battles of Concord and Bunker Hill in 1775 proved that the less experienced colonial troops were a force to be reckoned with. The next couple of years saw a series of successes and failures on both sides, but the turning point in the war came with an American victory in 1777 at the Battle of Saratoga. This encouraged the French to form a Franco-American alliance. The Spanish added their support in 1778 and the Netherlands followed suit in 1780.

European support reinforced America's morale, and although there were no decisive victories, they were able to hold out against the British until a stalemate was reached. American independence was finally obtained after the Battle of Yorktown in 1781 and the signing of the Treaty of Paris in 1783.

An American Rifleman in
the War of Independance

208 1776 THE WEALTH OF NATIONS

🎓 **FIRST PUBLISHED** in 1776, *The Wealth of Nations* (or *"An Inquiry into the Nature and Causes of the Wealth of Nations"*) was the greatest work of Scottish social philosopher and father of modern economics, Adam Smith.

Born in 1723 in Kirkcaldy near Edinburgh, Scotland, Smith studied social philosophy first at Glasgow University and then at Oxford. He became a teacher and in 1759 published the first of his two books, *The Theory of Moral Sentiments*.

In later life, he traveled and lectured abroad, mainly in France, rubbing shoulders with some of the greatest thinkers of the day.

Adam Smith (1723-1790)

On returning to England, he spent the next 10 years researching and writing *The Wealth of Nations*.

Published in the same year that America gained independence, Smith's most famous work promoted the theory that societies and nations are more productive and function best in a free market economy, where individuals use their own skills and capital without government interference.

The Wealth of Nations was the first modern work of economics and greatly influenced the newly independent America. It continues to be one of the most important works on economics ever published.

209 1776 WASHINGTON CROSSING THE DELAWARE

BY THE WINTER of 1776, George Washington's Continental army had suffered several defeats by the British during the American War of Independence. British troops under General William Howe had taken New York in November 1776 and American morale was at an all-time low. Encouraged by his victories and convinced there was little threat from the depleted American army, General Howe sent his troops into winter quarters at Trenton, New Jersey, leaving only a thin line of German mercenaries – the Hessians – to guard the banks of the Delaware River.

210 FAST FACT...

📖 **MARTHA WASHINGTON**
(wife of George) is the only woman whose portrait has appeared on a US bank note.

On the evening of Christmas Day 1776, Washington made the bold decision to lead 5000 of his troops across the frozen river. He crossed the Delaware to Trenton under cover of darkness and defeated the Hessians (still suffering from the excesses of their Christmas celebrations) in a surprise attack. The Crossing (also known as the Ten Crucial Days) and Washington's victory boosted American morale and led to subsequent victories at the second Battle of Trenton and Princeton, turning the course of the war.

General George Washington
(1732–1799)

211 1776 DECLARATION OF INDEPENDENCE

IN 1775, during the American Revolution, the Second Continental Congress sent an "Olive Branch Petition" to King George III of England in an attempt to avoid full-scale war. The petition was rejected and the King issued a "Proclamation of Rebellion," declaring the American colonies to be in a state of rebellion and calling upon the British Empire to suppress it.

This served to strengthen the American colonies' resolve to seek independence. In June 1776, over the course of 17 days, five members of the Continental Congress, including Benjamin Franklin, Thomas Jefferson and John Adams, drafted the "Declaration of Independence," justifying America's right to independence. It was presented it to Congress on July 1 and approved on July 4.

It became one of the most important documents in American history, declaring *"That these united Colonies are, and of Right ought to be Free and Independent States, that they are Absolved from all Allegiance to the British Crown, and that all political connection between them and the State of Great Britain, is and ought to be totally dissolved."*

July 4 continues to be celebrated as American Independence Day.

The signatures on the American Declaration of Independence, including John Hancock, Thomas Jefferson, Benjamin Franklin, John Adams, John Penn, and others

212 FAST FACT...

THE STATUE OF LIBERTY was a gift to the United States from the people of France. It is inscribed with the date July 4, 1776, the date of the Declaration of Independence.

213 FAST FACT...

THE WHITE HOUSE in Washington, DC, was originally gray. It was painted white to cover the smoke stains after it was burned in the war of 1812.

214 1781 THE SURRENDER OF YORKTOWN

DURING THE FINAL YEARS of the American War of Independence, America's Continental army had suffered a number of defeats. The British had captured Savannah in the Battle of Brewton Hill in December 1778 and had continued to fight along the Georgia-South Carolina border, forcing the Americans to surrender at the Siege of Charleston in 1780. By the August of 1780, the British, under General Lord Cornwallis, had secured another victory at Camden, South Carolina and the South was in their possession.

215 FAST FACT...

IN 1803, the US purchased Louisiana from France for just four cents an acre.

Meanwhile, American frontier guerrillas had been pursuing their own tactics and in October 1780, achieved a surprise victory over the British at the Battle of King's Mountain. This proved to be a pivotal event in the Southern campaign and forced Cornwallis to abandon his plans to invade North Carolina and retreat instead to Yorktown.

The French had by this time entered into an alliance with the Americans and on October 6, 1781, General Washington, together with French commander Comte de Rochambeau and their combined army and naval forces, moved to surround Cornwallis. With a French fleet preventing the British escaping by sea, Cornwallis was forced to surrender after a two-week siege and the American War of Independence was brought to an end.

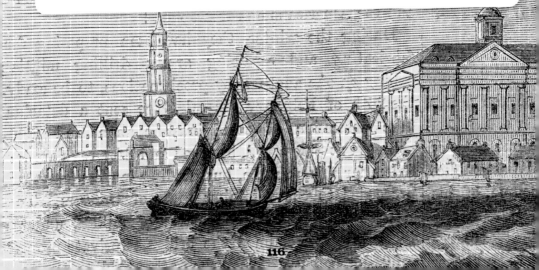

216 1782 MANIFESTO OF MISS WOLLSTONECRAFT

BORN ON APRIL 27, 1759 in London, England, Mary Wollstonecraft is considered to be one of the most important founders of feminist philosophy.

After enduring a difficult childhood with a drunk for a father, Mary left home and sought to educate herself. She read widely and took on work as a seamstress, governess, and lady's companion as a means to support herself. She was introduced into a circle of intellectuals including William Blake, Samuel Coleridge, and William Wordsworth, and worked for a while as reviewer and translator for the publisher Joseph Johnson.

Mary Wollstonecraft (1759–1797)

Always acutely aware of the inequalities within society, whether they were of class, age or gender, Mary wrote her first book, *A Vindication of the Rights of Men* on the subject of equality of opportunity, for which she received much criticism.

In 1792 she published her manifesto, *A Vindication of the Rights of Women*, in which she argued that the rights of man, which she had previously written about, also applied to women.

Her bold declarations earned her many enemies, but *A Vindication of the Rights of Women* went on to become a major influence in the fight for women's rights.

Charleston, USA

🎓 **THE UNITED STATES CONSTITUTION –** which became law on June 21, 1788, and was put into effect on March 4, 1789 – succeeded the Articles of Federation as America's governing document and changed the manner of governing from confederation to federal. It is the supreme law of the United States of America.

The Constitutional
Convention, Philadelphia

In May 1787, 55 state representatives met in Philadelphia for the Constitutional Convention. There were two plans to discuss: the Virginia Plan favored a central federal government with a House and a Senate, while the New Jersey Plan favored the main objectives of the Articles of Confederation plus equal representation for all states.

When the debate ended in a stalemate, the Connecticut Compromise (or the Great Compromise) was negotiated. It was eventually agreed that the House would represent the people, the Senate would represent the states and an Electoral College would elect a president.

The Constitution remains the oldest charter of supreme law in the world and has had considerable influence over many other constitutions across the world.

218 1789 GEORGE WASHINGTON ELECTED FIRST PRESIDENT

BORN ON FEBRUARY 22, 1732 on his father's plantation in Virginia, George Washington became a surveyor at the age of 16 and went on to map out Belhaven, Virginia. He played a role in the French-Indian War and by the age of 20 had been promoted to major. Retiring from the military in 1758, Washington went back to Virginia to manage the family estate at Mount Vernon and began to serve on the Virginian governing body known as the House of Burgesses. He prospered and became one of the wealthiest men in the state.

After being selected to represent Virginia at the Continental Congress, he was given the role of commander-in-chief of the Continental Army in 1775. During the American War of Independence he distinguished himself as a formidable leader and strategist.

Chosen to lead the Constitutional Convention in 1787, Washington was instrumental in developing the guidelines for a new federal government. In 1789 the Electoral College unanimously voted him first president of the United States.

Now regarded as the "Father of his country," Washington proved himself to be an inspired president who helped establish America as a nation in its own right.

A statue of General George Washington at the Boston Public Garden

Get that pigeon off me!

THE UNITED STATES

STATE	ADMISSION
Alabama (AL)	December 14, 1819
Alaska (AK)	January 3, 1959
Arizona (AZ)	February 14, 1912
Arkansas (AR)	June 15, 1836
California (CA)	September 9, 1850
Colorado (CO)	August 1, 1876
Connecticut (CT)	January 9, 1788
Delaware (DE)	December 7, 1787
Florida (FL)	March 3, 1845
Georgia (GA)	January 2, 1788
Hawaii (HI)	August 21, 1959
Idaho (ID)	July 3, 1890
Illinois (IL)	December 3, 1818
Indiana (IN)	December 11, 1816
Iowa (IA)	December 26, 1846
Kansas (KS)	January 29, 1861
Kentucky (KY)	June 1, 1792
Louisiana (LA)	April 30, 1812
Maine (ME)	March 15, 1820
Maryland (MD)	April 28, 1788
Massachusetts (MA)	February 6, 1788
Michigan (MI)	January 26, 1837
Minnesota (MN)	May 11, 1858
Mississippi (MS)	December 10, 1817
Missouri (MO)	August 10, 1821

STATE	ADMISSION
Montana (MT)	November 8, 1889
Nebraska (NE)	March 1, 1867
Nevada (NV)	October 31, 1864
New Hampshire (NH)	June 21, 1788
New Jersey (NJ)	December 8, 1787
New Mexico (NM)	January 6, 1912
New York (NY)	July 26, 1788
North Carolina (NC)	November 21, 1789
North Dakota (ND)	November 2, 1889
Ohio (OH)	March 1, 1803
Oklahoma (OK)	November 16, 1907
Oregon (OR)	February 14, 1859
Pennsylvania (PA)	December 12, 1787
Rhode Island (RI)	May 29, 1790
South Carolina (SC)	May 23, 1788
South Dakota (SD)	November 2, 1889
Tennessee (TN)	June 1, 1796
Texas (TX)	December 29, 1845
Utah (UT)	January 4, 1896
Vermont (VT)	March 4, 1791
Virginia (VA)	June 25, 1788
Washingon (WA)	November 11, 1863
West Virginia (WV)	June 20, 1863
Wisconsin (WI)	May 29, 1848
Wyoming (WY)	July 10, 1890

219 1799 DEATH OF QING EMPEROR QIANLONG

🎓 **THE FOURTH RULER** of the Qing Dynasty, Emperor Qianlong, was born in 1711, the fourth son of Emperor Yongzheng and the grandson of revered Emperor Kangxi. He ascended the throne at the age of 24, inheriting a prosperous and peaceful empire.

During the early years of his reign he proved himself to be a dedicated and inspired ruler who traveled his empire extensively. He was a successful military leader, succeeding in almost doubling the size of his empire with the annexing of Kazakhstan, Mongolia, parts of Siberia and the final subjugation of the nomadic tribes of Central Asia.

During the later years of his reign, Qianlong's judgment became impaired and he promoted a corrupt guardsman, Heshan, to the highest office in the empire. When Qianlong abdicated in 1795, not wishing to out-reign his grandfather, he continued to hold sway, but it was not until his death in 1799 that the extent of Heshan's corruption was revealed. The treasury was left severely depleted and the Qing Dynasty fell into a fatal decline.

Buildings in the Forbidden City in Bejing, China

220 1799 THE ROSETTA STONE

🎓 **ON JULY 21, 1798**, the French, under Napoleon Bonaparte, defeated the Egyptians at the Battle of the Pyramids. It was during the French occupation of Egypt that the study and science of Egyptology was founded and the most significant discovery in the field was made.

221 FAST FACT...

📖 **IF NAPOLEON** had been born a year earlier, he would have been Italian. He was born in Corsica in 1769, a year after it was bought by the French.

In July 1799, French solider, Pierre-François Bouchard, found an engraved block of basalt amongst the rubble of a demolished wall in the village of Rosetta. Weighing just under a ton, the inscriptions on the stone were in three different ancient scripts: Egyptian Hieroglyphics, Egyptian Demotic, and Greek. The Rosetta Stone was to provide the key to unlocking the language of Egyptian hieroglyphics.

In September 1799 the stone was moved to Cairo and a number of scholars, including Jean-François Champollion, began to work on deciphering the scripts. British scholar Thomas Young made great strides in deciphering the Demotic script, but it was Champollion who became the first to translate the stone in 1822.

When Napoleon was defeated by the British in 1801, the Rosetta Stone was shipped to England and is now housed at the British Museum, where it continues to be on display.

Napoleon Bonaparte
(1769–1821)

222 1805 BATTLE OF TRAFALGAR

🎓 **THE BATTLE OF TRAFALGAR** was a decisive naval battle that took place during the Napoleonic Wars.

The battle was the culmination of years of hostilities between the French and the British. When the short-lived Treaty of Amiens broke down in 1803, Britain once again declared war on France.

223 FAST FACT...

📖 *"[The Channel] is a mere ditch, and will be crossed as soon as someone has the courage to attempt it."* – Napoleon Bonaparte, 1803.

Emperor of France, Napoleon Bonaparte, determined to invade Britain but, only too aware of the might of the British navy, had to find a way of taking control of the English Channel in order to open up a clear passage for invasion. The French fleet allied with the Spanish and set sail for Cadiz, with plans to break through the British blockade of the Channel.

On October 21, 1805, off Cape Trafalgar on the Spanish coast, 27 ships of the British Royal Navy under Admiral Lord Nelson defeated the combined French-Spanish fleet under Admiral Pierre-Charles Villeneuve. Due to Nelson's unorthodox two column attack, it was the greatest sea battle of the time, with not a single British ship being lost. Nelson was mortally injured, but the victory destroyed Napoleon's invasion plans and allowed Britain to continue to dominate the seas for another hundred years.

224 FAST FACT...

📖 **USING SEMAPHORE** (a system of flags), Napoleon could send a message from Paris to Rome in under 4 hours.

225 FAST FACT...

📖 **AFTER HIS DEATH** at the Battle of Trafalgar in 1805, Admiral Nelson's body was shipped back to England in a barrel of brandy.

Nelson's flagship at the Battle of Trafalgar, HMS Victory

226 1810 THE MEXICAN WAR OF INDEPENDENCE

ON SEPTEMBER 16, 1810, a Catholic priest, Miguel Hidalgo y Costilla, from the town of Dolores, Mexico, declared war on the Spanish colonial government. The declaration, known as the Grito de Dolores (or Cry of Delores), marked the beginning of the Mexican War of Independence.

227 FAST FACT...

PIANIST Franz Liszt (1811– 1886) received so many requests for locks of his hair that he bought a dog and sent his admirers patches of its fur instead.

Costilla soon amassed a revolutionary army of peasant troops and marched on the mining city of Guanajuato, killing many of its Spanish defenders. Marching on towards Mexico City, the rebel army defeated the Spanish at The Battle of Monte de las Cruces, but failed to take Mexico City. They were pursued by the Spanish and defeated at the Battle of the Bridge of Calderon. Rebel leader Costilla was tried for treason and executed on July 31, 1811.

The push for Mexican independence continued with other peasant revolutionaries following Costilla's lead. But it was not until 1820, when a new liberal Spanish government called for reforms to appease Mexican rebels, that Royalists (Mexicans of Spanish descent wishing to maintain their privileged positions in Mexican society), led by Agustin de Iturbide, joined forces with insurgent commanders and entered Mexico City. The Spanish viceroy was forced to accept Mexican independence and signed the Treaty of Cordoba on August 24, 1821.

228 FAST FACT...

THE FIRST TIN CANS appeared in shops in 1810, but customers would have to wait another 50 years before the invention of the tin opener, using a lever-type opener in the meantime.

229 1815 NAPOLEON AT WATERLOO

AFTER A DISASTROUS attempt to invade Russia in 1812, Napoleon's Grande Armée was diminished, and by 1814 he was forced to surrender to the allies and abdicate. In May 1814, the Treaty of Paris restored Bourbon King Louis XVIII to the throne of France and Napoleon was exiled to the island of Elba, Italy.

230 FAST FACT...

IN 1815, news of the outcome of the Battle of Waterloo was brought from Belgium to England by carrier pigeon.

His exile was short-lived and by March 1815, he had escaped to the south of France and gathered a huge army of old supporters, who helped him reclaim the Imperial throne. The news of his return was not well received by his enemies – the alliance of Britain, Prussia, Austria and Russia – who immediately renewed their declaration of war upon him.

Napoleon knew his only choice was to attack before the allies had a chance to organize themselves.

On June 18, 1815, near Waterloo, Belgium, the French army under Napoleon met with the combined armies of the Seventh Coalition: British allies under the command of the Duke of Wellington and the Prussian army under the command of Gebhard von Blucher. The French army was overwhelmed and Napoleon suffered a humiliating defeat. He abdicated on June 22 and the Napoleonic wars were brought to an end by the signing of the Second Treaty of Paris on November 20, 1815.

231 FAST FACT...

AFTER the Battle of Waterloo, looters stole teeth from dead bodies to sell to rich people to use as false teeth.

Napoleon on his horse at the battle of Waterloo

232 FAST FACT...

"Next to a battle lost, the greatest misery is a battle gained." – The Duke of Wellington (1769–1852)

233 1819 PETERLOO MASSACRE

THE PETERLOO MASSACRE took place in St Peter's Field, Manchester, England on August 19, 1819. A crowd of around 60,000 people had gathered to protest against poverty and to demand the reform of parliamentary representation.

234 FAST FACT...

IN 1816, American statesman John Quincy Adams said: *"May our country be always successful, but whether successful or otherwise, always right."*

In the period following the Napoleonic Wars, England was suffering from political tensions and economic hardships. Only around two per cent of the population had the vote, unemployment was at a high, and many were on the brink of starvation – a situation aggravated by the introduction of the Corn Laws, which caused the price of bread to soar.

The Manchester Patriotic Union organized a peaceful demonstration to be held and invited radical reformer, Henry "Orator" Hunt to speak. Local magistrates panicked at the size of the gathering, sending in part-time cavalry to disperse the crowds and arrest the speakers.

The cavalry charged with sabers drawn and in the confusion and mayhem, 18 people were killed, , including a woman and child, and over 600 injured. The Manchester Guardian newspaper was established as a direct result of the massacre, but its long-term effects would lead to suffrage, the rise of the Chartist Movement and the development of the Trade Unions.

235 FAST FACT...

ON FEBRUARY 7, 1821, an American seal hunter named John Davis became the first human to set foot on the continent of Antarctica.

236 1821–1832 THE GREEK WAR OF INDEPENDENCE

🎓 **GREECE HAD BEEN** under oppressive Ottoman rule since the fall of the Byzantine Empire in 1453. Several attempts by the Greeks to gain liberty had failed but by 1814, inspired by the French Revolution, an underground organisation called *Filiki Eteria* (Friendly Union) had formed to gather together an army and weapons for a planned uprising.

237 FAST FACT...

📖 **LOUIS BRAILLE** developed his reading code for the blind in 1821, based on a system invented by a French army officer for night reading on a battlefield.

The first revolt in March 1821, led by General Aexandros Ypsylantis in the Danubian Principalities, failed but was quickly followed by an uprising in the Peloponnese Peninsula and the capture of Tripoli. Subsequent revolts in Central Greece, Crete and Macedonia were quashed, and the Turkish retaliation saw thousands of Greeks massacred.

As the revolution intensified, the Ottomans turned to Egypt for help and in 1825, an Egyptian army invaded and captured the Greek held Peloponnese.

In the meantime, the Greek insurrection had caught the attention of Britain, France and Russia, and on July 6, 1827, the three powers signed the Treaty of London, which called upon the Turks and the Greeks to end their hostilities. When the Ottoman Empire refused to accept the treaty, the European powers sent their naval fleets to Navarino Bay in October 1827 and defeated the Turkish and Egyptian fleets. Greece was finally given independent status in May 1832 after four further years of negotiation.

238 FAST FACT...

📖 **BEETHOVEN'S** 9th Symphony (1824) is one of the best-known works of Western classical music. He was stone deaf when he wrote it.

239 FAST FACT...

📖 **NAPOLEON,** who died in 1821, may have been killed by his wallpaper. It contained copper arsenite, which gives off toxic vapors when damp.

240 1822 THE BATTLE OF CARABOBO

IN THE EARLY 1800'S the population of Venezuela was divided between loyalty to Spain and a need for independence. When King Ferdinand VII of Spain was imprisoned following Napoleon's invasion, the move towards independence gathered momentum.

241 FAST FACT...

IN 1826, English chemist John Walker tried removing a blob of chemicals from a stick by scraping it on the floor, and accidentally invented the match.

242 FAST FACT...

IN 1826, German composer Felix Mendelssohn left the score of his latest work in a cab. Luckily, he was able to rewrite every note from memory.

243 FAST FACT...

SPANISH ARTIST Francisco de Goya, who died in 1828, may have been killed by his paint, which contained lead and mercury.

244 FAST FACT...

THE FIRST PERSON to survive a jump off Niagara Falls was 23-year-old Sam Patch, in 1829.

Leading supporter of the independence movement, Simon Bolivar, was instrumental in the founding of the First Venezuelan Republic in July 1811. However, after a disastrous earthquake in 1812, the Republic fell and the Spanish regained control of Venezuela.

Bolivar moved to Granada to recruit a new army. On his return to Venezuela in 1813, he marched into Caracas (the Admirable Campaign) and established the Second Venezuelan Republic. Once again the Spanish pushed him out and there followed years of civil war that devastated Venezuela.

In 1819, Bolivar launched a risky attack on Bogota, the Spanish headquarters of northern South America. Marching some 2500 troops across the Andes, he took Bogota by surprise and thus gained control of New Granada.

With his army now swollen with new recruits and captured weapons, Bolivar defeated the last Spanish Royalist force at the Battle of Carabobo and finally declared the new Republic of Gran Columbia, which included New Granada, Venezuela and Ecuador.

245 1832 THE GREAT REFORM ACT

THE ELECTORAL SYSTEM in England and Wales during the early nineteenth century allowed only a small percentage of the population to vote and had long been criticized as being unfair. The existence of "rotten boroughs" gave towns with a small electorate the right to elect two members to the House of Commons, whereas towns and cities that had experienced major population growth, such as Manchester, had no right to any parliamentary representation.

Previous calls for reform had failed. When Whig Prime Minister, Lord Grey, introduced The Reform Bill of 1831 into the House of Commons, it was defeated by the Tories, who were opposed to the idea of widening the electoral base. This sparked large-scale riots across England.

Fearing a revolution similar to that in France 1830, King William IV of England was persuaded by Grey to create new Whig peers, thus allowing the Reform Act of 1832 to be passed.

Although the Act did away with rotten boroughs and gave men with properties worth £10 the vote, it still left only one out of six males the right or means to vote.

246 FAST FACT...

LOUIS XIX was king of France for just 20 minutes on August 2, 1830 – the shortest reign in history.

247 FAST FACT...

WHEN THE FIRST RAILWAYS were built in the 1830's, some scientists warned that passengers would get nosebleeds at speeds over 15 mph.

248 FAST FACT...

A BRITISH ship arriving at a Chinese port in the 1830s fired its cannon in greeting, killing a member of the welcoming party.

249 FAST FACT...

THE FIRST railway accident occurred on June 17, 1831 when a boiler exploded on an American passenger train.

250 1836 THE ALAMO

IN THE EARLY 1820'S, American families had begun to settle in Texas – led by Stephen F. Austin, the "Father of Texas." At the time, Texas was part of the state of Mexico, and having just gained independence from Spain, Mexico was reluctant to give its colonists too much autonomy.

In 1833, Austin travelled to Mexico City to lobby for Texas's right to independence. Mexican president Santa Anna rejected his petition and Austin was arrested. By the time he was released in 1835, the revolt against the Mexican government had gathered momentum. By 1836, much of the Mexican army had been pushed out of Texas and a band of rebels, led by Colonel William Travis, had taken a defensive stand at the former Spanish mission, San Antonio de Valero, named "Alamo" after the Spanish word for the locally grown cottonwood. Hoping to quell any further acts of rebellion, Santa Anna stormed the Alamo on March 6, 1836, and executed all the rebels, including Davy Crockett.

A month later, the Texans retaliated and, encouraged by Major-General Sam Houston's cry of "Remember the Alamo!" they defeated 1250 Mexican troops at the Battle of Jacinto. On May 14, the Treaty of Velasco was signed granting Texas independence from Mexico.

251 FAST FACT...

AMERICAN writer Edgar Allen Poe was a poor soldier. He was thrown out of military academy in 1831 after committing 66 offenses.

252 FAST FACT...

ON SEEING the reformed British parliament in 1833, the Duke of Wellington remarked: *"I never saw so many shocking bad hats in my life."*

253 FAST FACT...

"Always be sure you are right, then go ahead." – Davy Crockett, US soldier, politician and folk hero, who died at the Battle of the Alamo, 1836.

254 FAST FACT...

IN 1837, a British judge ruled that if a man kissed a woman against her will, she was legally entitled to bite his nose off.

255 1839–42 THE FIRST OPIUM WAR

🎓 **IN THE EIGHTEENTH CENTURY,**
European and American demand for Chinese tea, silk, and porcelain grew rapidly. There was little the West could offer a pre-industrial China in return, causing there to be an imbalance in trade. In a bid to overcome this problem, the West traded their merchandise with Southeast Asia and India in exchange for raw materials, including opium, which could be used for trade with China.

The trade in opium proved to be extremely profitable and China was soon flooded with British imports. Demand for the drug increased, despite there being laws in place against its abuse and in spite of measures taken by the Qing government to prevent its import. In a bid to put an end to the illicit trade, the Qing Emperor ordered the seizure of all illegal opium imports. The destruction of over 20,000 chests of British opium worth millions of dollars, and the expulsion of foreign ships and merchants from Canton, triggered the first Anglo-Chinese War.

The British turned the full force of their superior navy on China. Fighting began on November 3, 1839 and by August 1842 the Qing Emperor had capitulated in a humiliating defeat.

256 FAST FACT...

📖 **SCOTTISH BLACKSMITH**
Kirkpatrick Macmillan created an early version of the pedal bicycle in 1839 – 24 years before it was officially invented.

257 FAST FACT...

📖 **THE PASTRY WAR** between France and Mexico began in 1838, when Mexico refused to pay for damage done by its army officers to a French restaurant in Mexico City.

An opium poppy, from which seeds are extracted

258 FAST FACT...

📖 **US PRESIDENT** William Henry Harrison died from pneumonia on April 4, 1841, just 32 days after taking office.

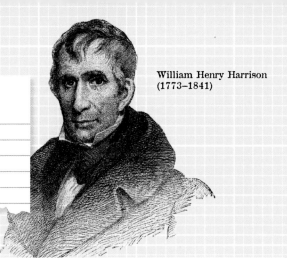

William Henry Harrison
(1773–1841)

259 1839 THE DURHAM REPORT

🎓 **THE DURHAM REPORT** was compiled by John George Lambton, 1st Earl of Durham, in response to rebellions against British rule in Upper and Lower Canada, which took place in 1837 and 1838.

260 FAST FACT...

📖 **THE WORLD'S** first postage stamps were issued in Britain in 1840.

The rebellions arose as a result of economic difficulties and a general dissatisfaction with the discriminatory policies of the British government, in particular with the Family Compact (a select group of public servants who remained loyal to Great Britain, shared a family bond and dominated government postings) in Upper Canada.

Durham travelled to Canada in May 1838 as newly appointed General Governor and High Commissioner of British North America. In his report, which he presented in 1839, he proposed three major changes: that Upper and Lower Canada be united into a single province, that a "responsible government" be established and that French-Canadians be assimilated into the English culture.

The uniting of Upper and Lower Canada laid the foundations for modern-day Canada, but the call for French assimilation proved to be highly controversial. His recommendation for a "responsible government" was initially rejected and did not come into force for another 10 years.

261 1842 THE TREATY OF NANKING

THE TREATY OF NANKING marked the end of the First Opium War. It was signed on August 29, 1842 aboard *HMS Cornwallis* between British government representative, Sir Henry Pottinger, and Chinese imperial commissioners Qiying, Yilibu, and Niujian.

It was the first of what were to be termed, "unequal treaties," as the terms of the treaty were solely in Britain's favor. The treaty stated that China should pay back the worth of the British opium destroyed during the war, that Hong Kong be ceded to Britain on a 99-year lease and that the ports of Shanghai, Guangzhou, Fuzhou, Xiamen and Ningbo be opened for foreign trade. British nationals in China were to be exempt from Chinese laws and Britain was to receive the same trading concessions as other countries. China viewed the terms of the treaty as a series of "national humiliations."

262 FAST FACT...

THE FAX machine was invented in May 1842 by Scottish craftsman Alexander Bain. It took another 140 years for it to become popular.

The treaty proved to be a disaster for the Chinese economy. With more ports open for foreign trade, the country was flooded with western goods, causing mass unemployment and riots within China. The treaty did not resolve the issue of the opium trade either, which was only addressed in the aftermath of the Second Opium War.

263 FAST FACT...

IN 1842, Mexican president Antonio de Santa Anna held a funeral for his own amputated leg.

THE FLAGSTAFF WAR (or Hone Heke's Rebellion) was fought between the Maori of New Zealand and the British Crown from March 1845 to January 1846 in the Bay Islands, New Zealand.

In 1840, after the colonization of New Zealand by the British, the founding document of New Zealand (the Treaty of Waitangi) was signed. It appointed a British governor, thereby establishing British law in New Zealand; it also gave the Maori tribes the right to keep their lands and maintain their culture.

However, the treaty was open to misinterpretation and British settlers soon began encroaching upon Maori lands. Hone Heke, leader of the Ngapuhi tribe and one of the original signatories of the Treaty of Waitangi, became increasingly disillusioned with the authority of the British. In March 1845, he and some of his men entered Kororareka and symbolically cut down the flagstaff flying the British flag, which Heke had himself had presented to the first British resident.

The Flagstaff War was initiated and grew into a three-way conflict between British forces and two factions of the Ngapuhi. It was marked by a number of engagements including the battles of Puketutu, Te Ahuahu, and Ohaeawai, but it was the inconclusive Battle of Ruapekpeka that finally ended the war in January 1846.

265 1845 UNITED STATES ANNEXES TEXAS

IN 1836, after the Republic of Texas had won independence from Mexico, American expansionists (led by President James K. Polk) called for the Republic to be admitted to the Union as a new state.

Mexico had never recognized Texan independence and it was feared that an annexation would lead to war. It was also feared that as Texas still tolerated slavery, the admittance of another slave state to the Union would cause an imbalance. But despite these misgivings, when it became clear that both Britain and France were making moves to ally with Texas, the United States acted swiftly and on December 29, 1845, Texas was annexed to the Union as the 28th state.

As feared, the Mexican government reacted badly and on May 1, 1846, Mexican troops laid siege to Fort Texas. They were quickly defeated by the Americans in the ensuing Battle of Palo Alto. The US officially declared war on Mexico on May 13, 1846. New Mexico was won by General Stephen Kearny and his "Army of the West," Mexico City was captured in August 1847 and a defeated Mexico finally agreed to peace with the signing of the Treaty of Guadaloupe on February 2, 1848.

266 FAST FACT...

A LAW passed in Britain in 1845 made attempted suicide a crime punishable by death.

267 1845–49 THE IRISH POTATO FAMINE

THE IRISH POTATO FAMINE (or the Great Famine) occurred in British-controlled Ireland in 1840–1849. Ireland had seen a massive rise in its population from some three million in the late 1700's to eight million by 1840 and was struggling to produce enough food. Many areas of agricultural land were controlled by absent English landlords, plus the prevailing system of land inheritance resulted in smaller and smaller sub-plots of land.

268 FAST FACT...

"Russia has two generals in whom she can confide – Generals Janvier (January) and Fevrier (February)." – Tsar Nicholas I of Russia (1796–1855)

The potato was an easy crop to grow and became the primary source of food until the appearance of a devastating fungus known as "the blight." The fungus instantly destroyed Ireland's main food supply, leading to widespread famine and the deaths of almost one million people. A further two million emigrated to Britain, the United States and Canada in a bid to escape what had become a ravaged country.

The British government were slow to respond and any relief operations bore little effect. The social, economic and political effects upon Ireland were catastrophic and centuries on, many believe that the confiscation of Irish land by the British – leaving too little land to feed the population – was a major cause.

269 FAST FACT...

"The Almighty indeed sent the potato blight, but the English created the Famine." – John Mitchel, Irish nationalist (1815–1875)

IRELAND.

ST PATRICKS, DUBLIN

LIMERICK CASTLE.

THE HOLY WELL

ROSS CASTLE, LAKE OF KILLARNEY.

ROUND TOWER, WICKLOW.

ATLANTIC OCEAN

IRISH SEA

NORTH CHANNEL

ULSTER

CONNAUGHT

LEINSTER

MUNSTER

SCALE

Longitude West from Greenwich

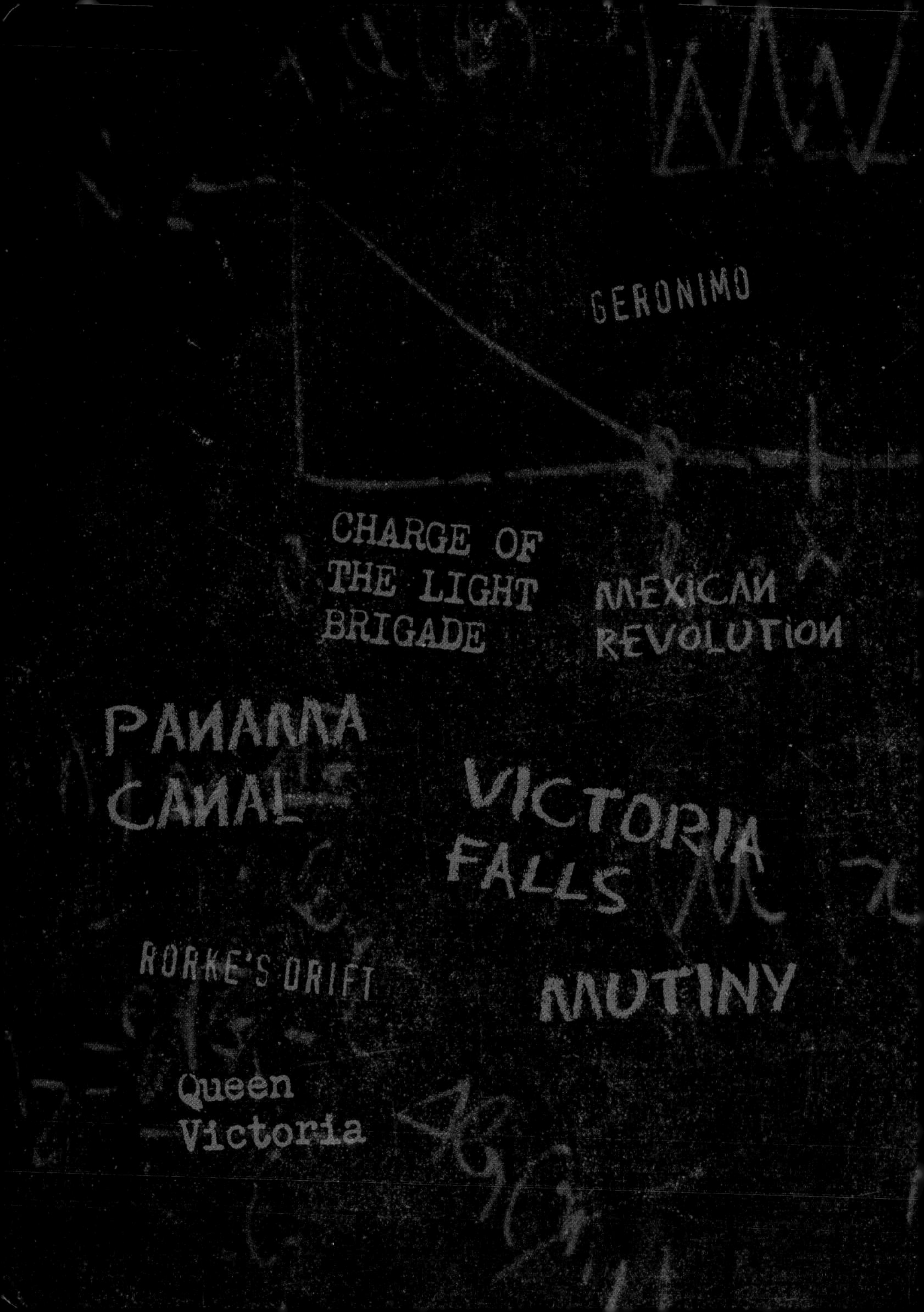

GERONIMO

CHARGE OF
THE LIGHT   MEXICAN
BRIGADE   REVOLUTION

PANAMA
CANAL   VICTORIA
                   FALLS

RORKE'S DRIFT   MUTINY

Queen
Victoria

BOXER UPRISING

GOLD RUSH

501

A Changing World

BATTLE OF SHILOH

TSAR OF RUSSIA

CUSTER'S LAST STAND

LINCOLN

emancipation

270 1849 THE GOLD RUSH

IN JANUARY 1848, while working to build a water mill, carpenter James Marshall discovered what he thought were flakes of gold in the American River, in the Sierra Nevada Mountains, California. John Sutter, owner of the mill, confirmed his suspicions and, although they tried to keep the discovery quiet, word soon got out and sparked the Gold Rush; one of the most significant events in early nineteenth-century American history.

271 FAST FACT...

IN 1853, Levi Strauss began making trousers for Californian gold miners using a tough blue material called denim. Jeans were born.

Before long, hundreds of thousands of gold-diggers were flooding to California to try their luck. They sailed in around Cape Horn or trekked along the California Trail and the Panama shortcut.

272 FAST FACT...

THE 1851 Great Exhibition in London's Hyde Park attracted over six million visitors, more than a third of Britain's population at the time.

Billions of dollars worth of gold was extracted and many "49ers" made their fortunes. Others were not so lucky and found only hardship, financial ruin and even death. As the gold-diggers ravaged the land, tens of thousands of Native Americans perished, losing homes and traditions and succumbing to diseases brought in by the prospectors.

The Gold Rush changed California significantly: towns and roads were built to accommodate the huge influx of people; new methods of transportation were developed and agricultural wealth grew as prospectors stayed to farm the land.

273 FAST FACT...

THE CRYSTAL PALACE, built to house the Great Exhibition, contained 293,655 panes of glass.

274 1852 NAPOLEON III BECOMES EMPEROR OF FRANCE

🎓 **NAPOLEON III,** or Louis Napoleon, was the nephew of the great general Napoleon Bonaparte, First Emperor of the French.

Born in Paris in 1808, Napoleon spent his early years in exile after his mother, Hortense de Beauharnais Bonaparte, was banished from France following the fall of Napoleon I.

From a young age, Napoleon dreamt of replicating the former glory and power of his famous uncle. After the death of his cousin Napoleon II, whose claim to be emperor was only recognized by "Bonapartists," Napoleon became head of the Napoleonic dynasty and in 1836 and 1840, made two unsuccessful attempts to claim the throne, for which he was imprisoned.

275 FAST FACT...

📖 **IN 1853,** US President Franklin Pierce was arrested for running over an old woman with his horse.

He escaped in 1846 and fled to England. He stayed until 1848, when he returned to France to make his third claim to the throne. With the country in political turmoil following the French Revolution, Napoleon promoted his Bonapartist policies and won a landslide electoral victory that saw him voted in as President.

276 FAST FACT...

📖 **WHEN AMERICAN** millionaire Cornelius Vanderbilt complained his French fries were too thick, his chef cut the next batch ultra-thin, thus inventing the potato chip!

277 1854 THE CHARGE OF THE LIGHT BRIGADE

THE CHARGE OF THE LIGHT BRIGADE took place on October 25, 1854 at the Battle of Balaclava, during the Crimean War. The charge was made against the Russian artillery by the British cavalry, consisting of the 17th Lancers, the 8th and 11th Hussars and the 4th and 13th Light Dragoons under the command of Major General the Earl of Cardigan, and a second unit (the Heavy Brigade) under the command of Major General James Scarlett.

278 FAST FACT...

IN 1854, Duke Cavendish-Scott-Bentinck built a vast underground network of rooms and tunnels beneath his estate, but never had a single guest.

The charge is variously described as one of the most heroic or unsuccessful events in British military history.

The British had taken the lead in battle when Cardigan received an order, apparently from Army Commander Lord Raglan, to attack the Russians. However, the meaning was misinterpreted in the confusion of the battlefield and resulted in Cardigan leading his troops to charge directly towards the Russian artillery. Forty per cent of the British cavalry were killed, but Cardigan was hailed as a hero for his bravery in facing the enemy and in his devotion to duty.

The episode was commemorated by Alfred Lord Tennyson in his famous poem *The Charge of the Light Brigade*.

279 FAST FACT...

AT THE hospital in Scutari, during the Crimean War, Florence Nightingale discovered that amputated limbs were left outside for pigs to eat.

280 1855 ALEXANDER II BECOMES TSAR OF RUSSIA

🎓 BORN IN MOSCOW

on April 17, 1818, Alexander II was the eldest son of Tsar Nicholas I. He became known as "Alexander the Liberator," due to the radical reforms he managed to implement during his reign as Tsar.

As a young man he was privately educated and put through the rigors of military training. Alexander ascended to the throne after the death of his father in 1855, a year before the signing of the Treaty of Paris brought the Crimean War to an end.

Alexander II of Russia (1818–1881)

Russia's defeat in the war highlighted the country's weaknesses. In response, Alexander sought to bring about major improvements by initiating reforms within education, transport, government, communications, and by abolishing the system of serfdom.

An autocratic leader, Alexander's reforms did not go far enough to satisfy many liberals who called for parliamentary democracy and freedom of expression. His suppressive policies provoked the formation of revolutionary terrorist organizations and, after escaping three assassination attempts, Alexander was killed on March 13, 1881 by a bomb thrown by a member of the People's Will movement.

145

281 1855 DAVID LIVINGSTONE DISCOVERS VICTORIA FALLS

DR DAVID LIVINGSTONE was a Scottish Congregationalist missionary and an explorer in southern and central Africa. He became one of the most popular national heroes in Victorian Britain because he completely lost contact with the outside world for six years and explored large swathes of previously uncharted regions of Africa.

282 FAST FACT...

KNOWN as "the dirtiest man in England," James Lucas never washed and his body turned black with grime. He became a national curiosity in the 1850s.

In November 1855, Livingstone sailed down the Zambezi River in order to view the sight the natives called "smoke that thunders." He became the first European to see the magnificent Mosi-oa-Tunya waterfall (in modern Zambia), which he renamed Victoria Falls.

In 1869, concerns for Livingstone's whereabouts prompted the *New York Herald* newspaper to send one of its reporters, Henry Morton Stanley, to locate him. Stanley finally found 56-year-old Livingstone on the shores of Lake Tanganyika in western Tanzania on October 27, 1871 and greeted him with the now famous line, "Dr Livingstone, I presume?" to which he replied, "Yes, and I feel thankful that I am here to welcome you."

The exchange may have been made up, since Stanley tore the relevant pages from his diary, but the witty remark relied on the fact that Livingstone was the only white person for hundreds of miles.

283 FAST FACT...

THE WORLD'S first roller coaster was a coal delivery railroad in Summit Hill, Pennsylvania. In the 1850's, people would pay to whizz down the steep track.

DRED SCOTT was an African-American slave, owned by US Army surgeon John Emerson, who lived in the pro-slavery state of Missouri.

When his owner was posted to the slave-free states of Illinois and Wisconsin, Scott went with him and spent many years living on "free soil."

After returning to Missouri in 1843, Emerson died. Encouraged by local abolitionists, Scott filed a suit against Emerson's widow for his right to freedom, claiming that as he had lived for years in slave-free states, he was entitled to be considered a free citizen.

285 FAST FACT...

📖 *"A house divided against itself cannot stand. I believe this government cannot endure permanently, half slave and half free."* – Abraham Lincoln, 1858

A Missouri court ruled against Scott and the case was taken to the United States Supreme Court. In March 1857, former slave-owner Chief Justice Roger B. Taney upheld a majority decision, which stated that as no black man, free or otherwise, had the right to US citizenship, they therefore had no right to sue in a federal court. The Missouri Compromise of 1820 (which prohibited slavery in certain territories) was declared unconstitutional as it violated the Fifth Amendment, which prohibited the government from depriving a person of their property (which included slaves) without due process of law.

Opponents of slavery were incensed by the decision and civil war loomed closer.

THE INDIAN MUTINY of 1857 (or India's First War of Independence) began when Indian troops of the East India Company's Bengal Army – already angered by the perceived threat to their traditional religious and social customs – were issued with the Pattern 1853 Enfield Rifles and cartridges. These rifles were rumored to be greased with pig and cow fat. The use of these particular animal fats was offensive to both Muslims and Hindus and the troops refused to use the cartridges, thus sparking a mutiny that quickly spread to include all 10 Bengal Light Cavalry Regiments, the 74 Bengal Native Infantry Regiments, and encouraged civilian rebellion across northern and central India.

Centered mainly in Delhi, the year-long mutiny was finally suppressed by the recapture of Delhi by British troops in 1858.

In the immediate aftermath of the mutiny, the Emperor of the Mughal Empire was deposed and exiled to Burma and the British East India Company was dissolved. The government of India was transferred directly to the British crown. The forming of the British Raj saw the election of a British general, or Viceroy, who represented the British Crown and ruled over India.

287 FAST FACT...

AS A PUNISHMENT during the Indian Mutiny, British officers would strap a rebel to the mouth of a cannon and fire it.

288 FAST FACT...

IN THE SUMMER of 1858, the stench of untreated sewage in London was so bad that Parliament had to close down.

289 1862 THE BATTLE OF SHILOH

IN 1862, during the American Civil War, the armies of Union General Ulysses S. Grant and Confederate General Albert Johnston clashed at Shiloh, Tennessee, in one of the bloodiest battles of the war.

After taking control of Nashville, Tennessee, Grant planned to continue his offensive on the Memphis and Charleston railroad in a bid to destroy the Confederacy's only supply route between the Mississippi Valley and the East coast. On April 6, 1862, while waiting for reinforcements at Shiloh on the Pittsburg Landing, he was advanced upon by over 50,000 Confederate troops in a surprise attack.

290 FAST FACT...

IN 1859, failed businessman Joshua Norton proclaimed himself Emperor of the United States. He even issued his own currency.

291 FAST FACT...

IN 1859, *The Saint Paul* was shipwrecked on the island of Rossel, Papua New Guinea, and all 326 passengers were eaten by cannibals.

The first day of battle saw the Confederate forces gaining ground, but at the loss of General Johnston. When Union reinforcements arrived on the second day, the exhausted Confederate Army was pushed into retreat at the cost of over 23,000 casualties.

Despite the Union victory, Grant was heavily criticized for being unprepared for the attack and the White House was called upon to remove him from his position as General. He was saved by the backing of President Lincoln, who is quoted as saying "I can't spare this man; he fights."

292 FAST FACT...

IN 1859, Thomas Austin released 12 rabbits on his estate in Victoria, Australia. Within 10 years the rabbit population numbered millions.

293 1862 EMANCIPATION PROCLAMATION

WHEN THE American Civil War first broke out in 1861, President Lincoln's main objective had been to keep the border slave states of Maryland, Missouri, Delaware, and Kentucky in the Union. Although anti-slavery himself, Lincoln did not wish to make the war a fight against slavery. To this end, the Crittenden Compromise was issued, which offered the reassurance that the Union had no plans to abolish the slave labor that the southern economy relied upon.

However, with the Union Army being swelled by fugitive slaves and on the back of a Union win at the Battle of Antietam in September 1862, Lincoln decided to issue the Emancipation Proclamation. Signed on September 22, 1862, the Proclamation outlawed slave-ownership in any Confederate state, exempting only border slave states that remained loyal to the Union.

The Proclamation strengthened Lincoln's Republican Party and in time, allowed for the 13th amendment to the US Constitution in 1865, which outlawed slavery throughout America.

The northern states acted adversely to the Proclamation, however, fearing that an influx of freed African-American workers would affect the labor market. Support for the war diminished to such a degree that in March 1863, the Union resorted to conscription.

294 FAST FACT...

THE WORLD'S first underground railway, the London Underground, was started in 1860.

295 FAST FACT...

CRINOLINES were the height of fashion in the 1860's. Some measured 5 feet 10 inches wide!

296 FAST FACT...

DURING the American Civil War, around 315 soldiers serving in the Union Army died of sunstroke.

297 FAST FACT...

AMERICAN Civil War general Stonewall Jackson had a notoriously bad sense of direction and was known for leading his men in circles.

298 1865 SURRENDER AT APPOMATTOX

ON APRIL 2, 1865, after four years of civil war, the Union Army (under General Ulysses S. Grant) finally drove the Confederate States Army (commanded by General Robert E. Lee) out of Petersburg following a nine-month campaign. Richmond fell to the Union.

General Lee retreated west, hoping to join with other Confederate forces in North Carolina. Stopping at Amelia Court House to collect supplies and food rations but finding little there, Lee was forced to delay his departure, giving Grant time to give chase. After clashing with Union troops at the Battle of Sayler's Creek and losing a quarter of his men, Lee headed to Appomattox station where he hoped supply trains were waiting. But outmaneuvered again, he arrived at Appomattox Court House on April 8, 1865 to find himself surrounded on three sides by Union cavalry. He had no choice but to admit defeat.

On the morning of April 9, 1865, General Lee and General Grant met in the house of Wilmer McLean to sign the surrender documents that brought to an end the Civil War, which had claimed over 600,000 lives.

299 FAST FACT...

SUSANNA M SALTER, America's first female mayor (1860–1), only discovered she was running when she saw her name on the slip in the voting booth.

300 FAST FACT...

WILLIAM BULLOCK, inventor of the web rotary printing press (1863), was also its victim. He was killed when he got caught up in one of the machines.

301 FAST FACT...

"We'll fight them, sir, 'til hell freezes over, and then, sir, we will fight them on the ice."
– A Confederate soldier at the Battle of Gettysburg, 1863.

302 FAST FACT...

"They couldn't hit an elephant at this dist..." – the last words of General John Sedgewick, killed in 1864 during the American Civil War.

303 1865 ASSASSINATION OF LINCOLN

IN 1864, well-known actor, John Wilkes Booth (a Confederate sympathiser) and eight other conspirators, plotted to kidnap President Lincoln and hold him hostage against the release of Confederate prisoners of war. However, a last-minute change of schedule for the President put paid to the scheme.

The following year, after Lincoln spoke out for the right of African-Americans to vote, Booth and his fellow conspirators renewed their plot. In a series of assassinations they planned to kill Lincoln and General Ulysses Grant at Washington's Ford Theater on April 14, 1865, where they were due to watch a production of *Our American Cousin*. Vice President, Andrew Johnson, and Secretary of State, William Seward, were to be killed later the same evening.

Unknown to Booth, General Grant had declined his invitation to the theater and thereby escaped his fate. Lincoln was not so lucky. After gaining access to the Presidential Box – unchallenged due to his status as an actor – Booth shot the president in the back of the head before escaping through the back of the theater. Lincoln died the following morning and Booth was tracked by Union soldiers and killed in Maryland.

Seward survived a vicious knife attack and Johnson was spared by the failed nerve of his would-be assassin.

304 FAST FACT...

"*Sic semper tyrannis! [Thus always to tyrants] The South is avenged.*" – John Wilkes Boothe, upon assassinating Abraham Lincoln, 1865.

Abraham Lincoln
(1809–1865)

305 1866 PRUSSIA DEFEATS AUSTRIA IN SEVEN WEEKS WAR

🎓 **THE SEVEN WEEKS WAR,** or the Austro-Prussian War, was fought between the German Confederation, led by the Austrian Empire and its German allies, and Prussia with its German allies and Italy, on June 14– August 23, 1866.

Otto Von Bismarck
(1815–1898)

War broke out at the instigation of the powerful German statesman Otto von Bismarck, who accused the Austrians of violating the Convention of Gastein. He used this pretext to forge ahead with Prussia's longterm aim to unify Germany under Prussia's Hohenzollern Dynasty and to expel Austria from the Confederation. To aid his plan, Bismarck made a secret military alliance with Italy, which had long wanted to regain Venetia from Austria.

Although Italy was defeated in its attempt to seize Venetia, its participation in the war forced Austria to split its forces, and the Prussian Army went on to score an overwhelming victory over Austria and its allies on July 3 at the Battle of Koniggratz.

The war was concluded by the signing of the Treaty of Prague in August 1866, by which Austria agreed to the dissolution of the German Confederation; enabling Prussia to form the North German Confederation.

306 FAST FACT...

📖 **ALFRED NOBEL**, who invented dynamite in 1867, went on to establish the Nobel Prize.

307 1869 THE SUEZ CANAL OPENS

THE SUEZ CANAL, or the "Highway to India," is an artificial waterway located in Egypt that connects the Mediterranean Sea to the Gulf of Suez, a northern extension of the Red Sea.

During the late 1700's, Napoleon Bonaparte had investigated the possibility of constructing a French-controlled canal, but engineering errors forced the plans to be abandoned. It was not until 1858, when Egyptian Viceroy Said Pasha appointed French engineer Ferdinand de Lesseps to head the project, that the Universal Suez Ship Canal Company was formed and building of the waterway could begin.

The Suez Canal took 10 years to finish at a cost of one hundred million dollars. A magnificent feat of engineering, it was officially opened by French Empress Eugenie on November 17, 1869 from the Imperial yacht, *Aigle*.

The finished canal was 101 miles long and 26 feet deep. It had an immediate impact on worldwide trade, allowing goods to be shipped around the globe at speed. During the Constantinople Convention of 1888, it was agreed the canal should always be free and open, "in time of war as in time of peace, to every vessel of commerce or of war, without distinction of flag."

It is now owned by the Suez Canal Authority of the Arab Republic of Egypt.

Ferdinand De Lesseps in the Dutch consulate of Alexandria, Egypt.

308 1870 THE UNIFICATION OF ITALY

DURING THE EARLY nineteenth century, Italy consisted of a jumble of states under the various rule of Spain, France, Germany, and Austria and had no political, economical, or cultural cohesion.

With the unification of Italy as a goal, Victor Emmanuelle II, king of the state of Piedmont (Sardinia), and his Prime Minister, Camillo Cavour, set about reorganizing and developing the region into a powerful state. Knowing that he would need outside assistance to overcome internal resistance, Cavour sent his forces to fight with the French and British against Russia in the Crimean War of 1854–56. In doing so, he won the friendship of Napoleon III and the support of France during the 1859 second Italian War of Independence, which resulted in the northern and central states of Italy unifying with Sardinia. Italy's *Risorgimento* (resurrection) had truly begun.

With the intervention of revolutionary leader Giuseppe Garibaldi and his army of "Red Shirts," Sicily was invaded, the Bourbons were overthrown and southern Italy was liberated.

When Italy sided with Prussia in the Austro-Prussian War, it won back Venice from Austria and by 1871, after claiming Rome back in the aftermath of the Franco-Prussian War, Italy was finally unified.

Italian patriot
Giuseppe Garibaldi
(1807- 1882)

309 1870–71 FRANCO-PRUSSIAN WAR

THE FRANCO-PRUSSIAN WAR, or Franco-German War, was fought between France and Prussia in 1870–71.

310 FAST FACT...

WHEN PARIS ran out of food during the siege of 1870–1, restaurants began serving cat, dog, and rat.

Following French losses during the Austro-Prussian War of 1866, Napoleon III, Emperor of France, was keen to regain some prestige in Europe and was alarmed by the proposed Prusso-Spanish alliance when the vacant throne of Spain was offered to Leopold, a member of the Hohenzollern dynasty. Napoleon demanded that Leopold's candidacy be withdrawn. Leopold complied but Napoleon pushed further and demanded an apology. In a move calculated to precipitate a war, Prussian chancellor Otto von Bismarck published Napoleon's communications in what came to be known as the Ems Dispatch. Bismarck hoped to rid Germany of French influence as part of his ongoing plan to unify Germany under Prussian control.

France declared war on July 19, 1870 but could only mobilize 200,000 troops against Prussia's 400,000. France lost a number of conflicts and on September 2, 1870, at the Battle of Sedan, Napoleon and his army were captured. The French declared a Third Republic and the war continued until the Prussians finally defeated the French at the Siege of Paris on January 28, 1871. The German Empire was declared and the Treaty of Frankfurt was signed on May 10, 1871.

311 FAST FACT...

OSCAR WILDE'S two half-sisters burned to death at a party in 1871 when they walked too close to a fire and their crinolines caught alight.

312 FAST FACT...

IN 1875, Thomas Edison accidentally discovered photocopying while using paraffin to try and improve telegraph tape.

313 1876 CUSTER'S LAST STAND

THE BATTLE OF LITTLE BIGHORN, Custer's Last Stand or the Battle of Greasy Grass, is the most famous battle in the Great Sioux War of 1876, fought over land and recently discovered gold. It took place near the Little Bighorn River in eastern Montana territory, near present-day Crow Agency, Montana.

General Custer had been ordered to wait for reinforcements at the mouth of the Little Bighorn River before attacking, but on sighting Chief Sitting Bull nearby, he grew impatient and led his men to attack.

314 FAST FACT...

THE ONLY survivor from the losing side at the Battle of Bighorn was a horse named Comanche.

Custer's force of 650 men, a battalion of the US Seventh Cavalry Regiment, met 4000 Cheyenne and Sioux warriors led by Crazy Horse and Sitting Bull. Custer had underestimated the numbers of his enemy. He suffered a severe defeat on Last Stand Hill, five of the Seventh's companies were annihilated and Custer was killed. Native American accounts said the fighting against Custer lasted only "as long as it takes a hungry man to eat a meal," and noted that several soldiers committed suicide near the end of the battle.

General Custer (1839–1876) at the Battle of Little Bighorn

315 1876 QUEEN VICTORIA BECOMES EMPRESS OF INDIA

📖 **FOLLOWING THE INDIAN MUTINY** of 1877 and dissolution of the British East India Company, the British Raj was formed and India was incorporated into the British Empire.

Queen Victoria unsurprisingly endorsed the expansion of the Empire and proclaimed that the move "should breathe feelings of generosity, benevolence and religious toleration."

In 1876, British Parliament, under the encouragement of British Conservative Prime Minister Benjamin Disraeli, passed the Royal Titles Act or, to give it its full name, "An Act to enable Her most Gracious Majesty to make an addition to the Royal Style and Titles appertaining to the Imperial Crown of the United Kingdom and its Dependencies."

In a bid to tie Britain even more closely to India, the Act officially recognized Queen Victoria as Empress of India. The passing of the act faced some opposition from Liberals who saw the title as being too closely associated with absolutism.

Nevertheless, on January 1, 1876 during celebrations at the Imperial Assemblage in Dehli, it was announced by Viceroy Lord Lytton that Her Majesty Queen Victoria had assumed the title of Empress of India.

316 FAST FACT...

📖 **ALEXANDER** Graham Bell is the inventor of the telephone – but only just. He beat his rival Elisha Gray to the patent office by one hour.

317 FAST FACT...

📖 **IN 1877,** Thomas Edison invented the music-playing phonograph. In the same year, Chester Greenwood invented earmuffs!

318 FAST FACT...

📖 **AUSTRALIAN** outlaw Ned Kelly dressed in home-made metal armor during a shootout with the police. It did not prevent him getting killed.

319 FAST FACT...

📖 **THE SHORTEST** street in the world is Ebenezer Place in Wick, Scotland. It is just 6 feet 6 inches long and contains one address: 1 Ebenezer Place.

320 1879 RORKE'S DRIFT, THE ANGLO-ZULU WAR

IN 1877, British colonial administrator Sir Bartle Frere was charged with the task of unifying South Africa's colonies and independent black states into a Confederation of South Africa.

Realizing that the only thing standing the way of this unification was the might of the Zulu Kingdom, he initiated a war without the full backing or knowledge of Benjamin Disraeli's British government.

On January 11, 1879, following the Zulu king Cetshwayo's rejection of an unacceptable ultimatum from Frere, a 5000-strong British force led by Lord Chelmsford marched to Rorke's Drift, Zululand to confront the Zulus.

Totally underestimating the fighting and tactical prowess of the Zulu warriors and hampered by incompetent leadership and ambiguous orders, the British forces were overrun by the Zulus in the Battle of Islandlwana on January 22, 1879. British losses were horrendous with 1350 out of the original 1750 British soldiers being killed.

Later the same day, a small British garrison stationed at Rorke's Drift managed, over the course of 12 hours, to fight off over 3000 Zulu warriors. Much was made of this heroic defence in an effort to direct attention away from the unnecessary losses made at Islandlwana. The British government awarded an unprecedented 11 Victoria Crosses and the event was immortalised in the 1964 film *Zulu*.

321 FAST FACT...

"Last words are for fools who haven't said enough." – the last words of German philosopher and economist Karl Marx, who died in 1883.

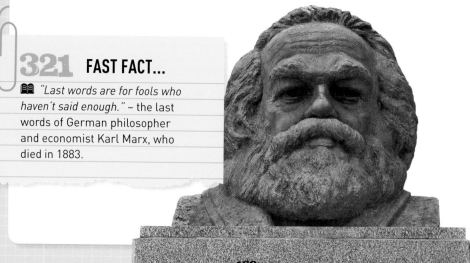

160

WORKERS OF ALL LANDS

The cocaine plant

322 FAST FACT...

📖 **COCA COLA,** invented in 1885, originally contained wine and cocaine and was sold as a medicine.

323 1880–1914 THE PANAMA CANAL

🎓 **THE PANAMA CANAL** is a 50 mile-long artificial waterway that passes across the Isthmus of Panama in Central America to link the Atlantic Ocean to the Pacific Ocean. Building of the canal took 34 years to complete and became the most expensive private venture in recent history.

In 1869, the French obtained an agreement from the Columbian government to begin work on the proposed waterway. Following his success with the Suez Canal, French engineer Ferdinand de Lesseps was put in charge of the scheme. The Panama Canal Company was formed and over 400 million dollars was raised from private investors.

The project was overwhelmed with problems from the onset: engineering errors, a massive underestimation of costs and completion time, mudslides, floods and tropical diseases, which killed over 22,000 workers between 1881–1889. When news of these difficulties reached the shareholders, stocks plummeted and in 1889 the company was declared bankrupt.

The project lay dormant for 15 years until in May 1904, the United States and the newly independent Panamanians signed the Hay-Bunau-Varilla Treaty and America took control of the Panama Canal Zone for 10 million dollars.

The canal was finally completed in 1914, reducing the journey time between the Atlantic and Pacific oceans by more than a half.

324 1886 AMERICAN TROOPS CAPTURE GERONIMO

BETWEEN 1849–1886, American troops were involved in a series of conflicts with the various Apache tribes of native America. When American and Mexican settlers began encroaching on the traditional Apache lands, which stretched from southern California to western Texas and northern Arizona to Mexico, the Apaches retaliated by raiding the settlers' camps. This often resulted in bloodshed.

325 FAST FACT...

IN 1888, an Egyptian farmer found an ancient cemetery containing 10,000 cat mummies. They ended up being ground into fertilizer.

One of the most notorious Apache warriors of the time was Geronimo, a member of the Chiricahua Apache. After his family was murdered by Mexican soldiers in 1858, he began to lead revenge raids on Mexican settlements. Captured by American troops in 1883, Geronimo surrendered and agreed to settle on the San Carlos Indian Reservation.Two years later however, he escaped to Mexico and resumed his raids on Mexican settlements.

Geronimo was ruthlessly pursued during the summer of 1886 by General Nelson Miles. He finally surrendered at Skeleton Canyon in 1886 and was later sent to Florida where he lived to old age and became an unlikely celebrity.

326 FAST FACT...

THE EIFFEL TOWER, completed in 1889, contains 18,038 pieces of iron, held together by 2.5 million rivets.

327 1890 CECIL RHODES ESTABLISHES RHODESIA

BORN IN HERTFORDSHIRE in 1853, British imperialist Cecil Rhodes was sent at the age of 17 to live with his brother Herbert in South Africa, in the hope that the warmer climate would calm his asthma.

328 FAST FACT...

IN THE 1890S, Ethiopian emperor Menelek bought 3 electric chairs from the USA. The was only one problem: Ethiopia had no electricity at the time.

He returned to England briefly to attend Oxford University, but by this time he was already well on the way to making his fortune in South Africa, having opened the Kimberley diamond fields in partnership with his brother. In 1880 he formed the DeBeers Mining Company which, by 1891, owned 90% of the world's diamond mines.

Rhodes fostered ambitions to see British rule established in Africa from "the Cape to Cairo." With this ambition in mind, and making use of his personal fortune, he joined the Parliament of Cape Colony in 1881 and became prime minister in 1890.

He was a key player in the Jameson Raid of December 1895 and as a result was forced to resign as prime minister. He went on to establish the British South Africa Company, which received a Royal Charter in 1889, enabling him to claim land in the Zambesia territories. In May 1895, these colonies were renamed in his honor. It was not until a new constitution was established in 1980 that Rhodesia became modern-day Zimbabwe.

329 FAST FACT...

In 1890, Eugene Schieffelin released 60 starlings, a non-native bird, in New York. Today there are over 2 million starlings in North America.

330 1898 SPANISH-AMERICAN WAR BREAKS OUT

IN THE LATE nineteenth century, a growing number of American expansionists called for the United States to fulfil its "Manifest Destiny," a belief made popular by the journalist John O'Sullivan, who stated that the US was destined to "overspread and to possess the whole of the continent."

331 FAST FACT...

IN 1893, New Zealand became the first country to give women the vote.

America had been keeping a close eye on Cuba during the Cuban War of Independence against Spain, and public pressure for US intervention was whipped up when newspaper giants, the *New York World* and the *New York Journal*, published exaggerated reports of Spanish atrocities in Cuba. In January 1898, the USS *Maine* was sent to Havana to guard American interests. It was sunk in an explosion thought to be caused by Spanish mines. American newspapers reacted strongly to the news that 266 American sailors had perished, and published the headlines, "Remember the Maine! To hell with Spain!"

American president William McKinley tried to pursue a diplomatic resolution, but war with Spain became inevitable. After three months of fighting, the US won control of Cuba, Wake Island, the Philippines, Puerto Rico and Guam, and had the beginnings of a Pacific Empire.

332 FAST FACT...

THE SHORTEST WAR in history was fought between Britain and Zanzibar in 1896. Zanzibar surrendered after 38 minutes.

333 FAST FACT...

IN 1894, distinguished scientist Lord Kelvin declared that radio had no future and that heavier-than-air flying machines were impossible.

334 FAST FACT...

"The report of my death was an exaggeration." – Mark Twain, 1897.

336 1899 THE HAGUE CONVENTION

🎓 **THE HAGUE CONVENTION** of 1899 was an international peace treaty negotiated at The Hague in the Netherlands. The Hague Peace Conference was instigated by Russian Tsar Nicholas II and his foreign minister Mikhail Nikolayevich in the hope of laying down international laws to limit warfare and to discuss arms limitations.

Twenty-six countries attended the conference, held from May 18, 1899 until the signing of the Convention on July 29, the same year. The treaty went into force on September 4, 1900.

The conference was considered a success. The Court for the Pacific Settlement of International Disputes was established and the most contentious methods of war were banned. These included the launching of missiles from balloons, the use of hollow point bullets (which flatten in the human body), and the use of asphyxiating or injurious gases.

A Second Conference was called by Theodore Roosevelt in 1907, but failed to achieve a unanimous vote to create an international court for compulsory arbitration. Germany was one of the few countries that vetoed the idea.

The Hague Conventions were to influence the later development of the League of Nations and the Geneva Conventions in helping to formalize the laws of war and war crimes.

337 1900 US ANNEXES PUERTO RICO

AMERICA INVADED Puerto Rico on July 25, 1898, during the Spanish-American War. The island fell easily and was occupied by US troops under the command of General Nelson Miles. When the 1898 Treaty of Paris formally concluded the war, America was given colonial authority over Puerto Rico, Guam and the Philippines.

On April 12, 1900, the Foraker Act (or the Organic Act of 1900) was passed by the Fifty-Sixth Congress in order to attach Puerto Rico to the US as an unincorporated territory and to establish civilian government on the island.

The new government consisted of an American-appointed governor and an executive council, a House of Representatives with 35 elected members and a Supreme Court. A two-house legislature consisted of a popularly elected lower house and a US-appointed upper chamber. The first governor of the island, Charles H. Allen, was inaugurated on May 1, 1900.

Residents of the island were to be considered citizens of Puerto Rico and not US citizens. Following an independence movement in 1909, the 1917 Jones Act was passed which proclaimed Puerto Rico to be an, "organized but unincorporated territory," and gave its inhabitants the right to US citizenship.

El Morro Castle
in Old San Juan,
Puerto Rico

338 1900–01 BOXER UPRISING IN CHINA

SINCE THE OPIUM WARS of 1839–1842 and 1856–1860, China had been forced to tolerate excessive demands from the West for trading and extra-territorial rights. Large sections of the Chinese population began to resent the Western influence on their culture and the Qing Dynasty for its apparent weakness and inefficiency in resisting European demands.

Anti-foreign feelings spread as China's industries suffered under an influx of cheap western goods. Unemployment levels rose and the Chinese government was forced to raise taxes, adding to the economic plight of the Chinese people.

339 FAST FACT...

THE WORLD'S first facelift was performed by Eugene Hollander on a Polish aristocrat in 1901.

Anti-European secret societies began to form, one of which was the I-ho-ch'uan, dubbed the "Boxers" due to the fact that many of its male members practised boxing as a form of self-defence.

The Boxers initiated violent campaigns against westerners and westernized Chinese. By 1899, they were massacring European missionaries and the rebellion had spread to Peking. Not wanting to be seen as pro-foreign, the Qing Dynasty had no choice but to support the uprising.

In order to protect their interests in China, an international force comprising Americans, Russians, French, British, Italians, and Japanese was dispatched and the Boxers and the Qing army were soon defeated.

Peace was established with the Boxer Protocol, signed in September 1901.

340 FAST FACT...

IN 1904, a tea merchant sent out some samples in little silk bags. His customers placed the bags in their cups, accidentally inventing the teabag.

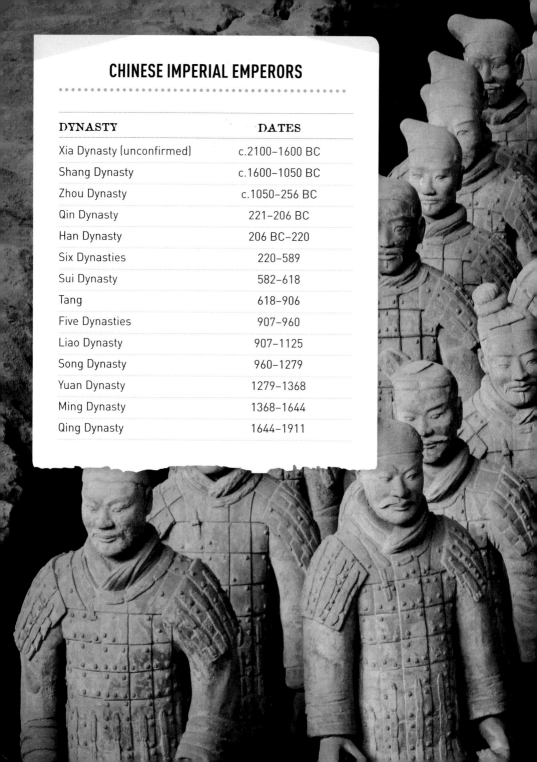

CHINESE IMPERIAL EMPERORS

DYNASTY	DATES
Xia Dynasty (unconfirmed)	c.2100–1600 BC
Shang Dynasty	c.1600–1050 BC
Zhou Dynasty	c.1050–256 BC
Qin Dynasty	221–206 BC
Han Dynasty	206 BC–220
Six Dynasties	220–589
Sui Dynasty	582–618
Tang	618–906
Five Dynasties	907–960
Liao Dynasty	907–1125
Song Dynasty	960–1279
Yuan Dynasty	1279–1368
Ming Dynasty	1368–1644
Qing Dynasty	1644–1911

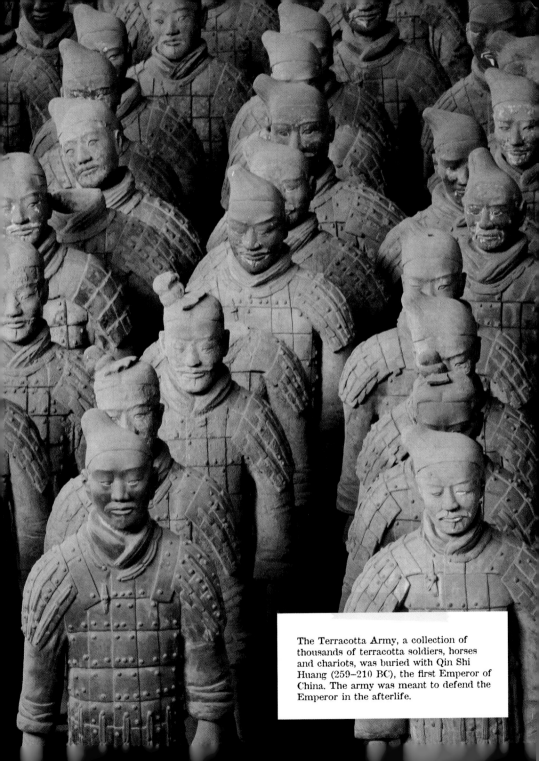

The Terracotta Army, a collection of thousands of terracotta soldiers, horses and chariots, was buried with Qin Shi Huang (259–210 BC), the first Emperor of China. The army was meant to defend the Emperor in the afterlife.

341 1904–05 RUSSO-JAPANESE WAR

DURING THE EARLY 1900'S, both Russia and Japan shared ambitions for expansion into the Far East. Japan had already won Formosa and Port Arthur from the Chinese Empire during the Sino-Japanese War of 1894–95, but had later been forced by European intervention to relinquish Port Arthur. To add to Japan's humiliation, the Triple Intervention (between Russia, Germany, and France) allowed Russia to lease Port Arthur and the surrounding Liaotung Peninsula, thus establishing a strategic Far East naval base.

The Japanese were further angered by Russia's failure to remove its troops from Manchuria after assisting China in the Boxer rebellions, and by growing tensions in Korea where both Japan and Russia had interests.

Fuelled by these grievances, on February 8, 1904, the Japanese Navy launched an attack on the Russian fleet at Port Arthur. The Russians were defeated at the Siege of Port Arthur and at the later battles of Sandepu, Mukden, and Tsusima.

Russia's confidence was severely dented and with the added difficulty of the Russian Revolution to contend with, Tsar Nicholas II agreed to sign the Treaty of Portsmouth in August 1905. The treaty ended the conflict, with Russia agreeing to recognize Korea as a Japanese sphere of interest and with Japan also receiving the Liaotung Peninsula and the South Manchurian Railway.

Antique illustration of
a ship convoy sailing
through the Suez canal.

342 1904 ENTENTE CORDIALE

🎓 **THE ENTENTE CORDIALE** was an agreement or declaration of friendship between Britain and France. Signed on April 8, 1904, the agreement was intended to establish a diplomatic understanding between the two countries and to put an end to long-standing colonial disputes.

The Entente comprised three sections. The first was a promise by the French that they would not challenge British control in Egypt, and in return Britain would allow France to preserve its interests in Morocco. Free passage through the Suez Canal was also guaranteed. In the second section, France gave up its rights to the western coast of Newfoundland (excluding fishing rights), and Britain gave the French Yarbutenda in the Gambia to use as a trading post, and the Iles de Los in Guinea. In the final section, Britain promised to recognize French influence in Siam (modern-day Thailand) to the east of the River Menam's basin, while the French promised to recognize British influence to the west of the basin.

The Entente Cordiale was not an alliance as such, as the two nations did not pledge to provide military support to one another. But it was a powerful document which to this day remains a significant factor in the diplomatic history of both France and Britain.

343 1905 THE POTEMKIN

THE POTEMKIN was a battleship in the Russian Navy's Black Sea Fleet. During the Russian Revolution of 1905, the *Potemkin* was out at sea on maneuvers, under the command of Captain Golikov. On June 14, 1905, the crew refused to eat poor-quality meat, which was apparently crawling with maggots. The exact details of what happened next are unclear, but it is certain that a confrontation between the crew (headed by Grigory Vakulenchuk), Captain Golikov and his second-in-command, Ippolit Giliaroysky, ended in the death of Vakulenchuk and pushed the crew to mutiny.

Seven of the ship's officers, including Captain Golikov and Giliaroysky, were thrown overboard or killed, while quartermaster Afanasy Matushenko took over command.

Late that evening, the *Potemkin* sailed into Odessa where the crew hoped to take advantage of the revolution and garner the support of the striking Russian workers. When the body of Vakulenchuk was laid out on the Odessa steps, a large crowd of revolutionaries gathered. By evening, clashes between demonstrators and troops had ended in violence and bloodshed when the *Potemkin* fired two shells into the city.

When two Russian battleships ordered to sink the *Potemkin* refused to fire, the mutinous ship escaped out to sea and sailed to Constanta, where it was handed over to the Romanian authorities.

344 FAST FACT...

IN 1906, William Kellogg forgot about a pot of wheat he had left heating on the stove. He tried flattening the dried-out wheat, and invented the cornflake.

345 FAST FACT...

IN 1905, 11-year-old Frank Epperson left a stirrer in his glass of lemonade. By morning it had frozen solid. He had invented the ice pop.

346 1906 FIRST ELECTED RUSSIAN PARLIAMENT

IN THE EARLY 1900'S, during the reign of Tsar Nicholas II, the people of Russia were desperate for reform. Events such as Bloody Sunday and the Potemkin Mutiny epitomized the feeling of unrest during the 1905 Revolution.

Under the advice of his Chief Minister Sergi Witte, the Tsar published the October Manifesto which promised "freedom of conscience, speech, assembly and association." He also announced the formation of Russia's first parliament, the State Duma.

The electoral laws allowed males over the age of 25 to vote, including peasants and gentry but excluding soldiers and officers. The general elections took place in March 1906 and among the parties formed were the Trudoviks, the Octobrists, and the Union of Land-Owners.

Before the First Duma could meet, the government issued the Basic Law of 1906, which downgraded the Duma to below the State Council of Imperial Russia, which had been in existence as a legislative body since 1810. The Tsar, determined to keep hold of his autocratic rule, gave himself the right to choose members of the Council and to dissolve the Duma if he chose.

The First Duma met in the Taurida Palace in St Petersburg in May 1906. The Tsar rejected all proposals put to him and the Duma was dissolved in the July. It was to be convened a further four times before the collapse of the Empire in 1917.

347 FAST FACT...

NICHOLAS II was the last emperor of Russia. He and his family were shot dead by Bolsheviks in 1918.

348 1908 COMET STRIKE AT TUNKGUSKA

At about 7:15 AM on June 30, 1908, a massive explosion occurred near the Podkamennaya Tunguska River in what is now Krasnoyarsk, Russia. The force of the explosion was so powerful that it flattened over 80 million trees in a 1336 square mile area and its effect was felt over 1000 miles away in London.

As the area was so remote at that time, it was another 10 years before the first scientific expedition was able to explore the region and find out the cause of the blast.

The expedition was led by Leonid Kulik, a Russian mineralogist, who on seeing the impact area for the first time wrote, "The results of even a cursory examination exceeded all the tales of eyewitnesses and my wildest expectations."

It is thought that a meteorite or comet fragment exploding 5–10 kilometres (3–6 miles) above the earth's surface could have caused an air burst, which is estimated to have been a thousand times more powerful than the Hiroshima atomic bomb.

Kulik was never able to establish the true cause of the Tunguska event and to this day the exact cause remains a mystery.

349 FAST FACT...

📖 **IN 1909,** Louis Bleriot became the first man to fly from England to France. His wooden plane was held together with piano strings.

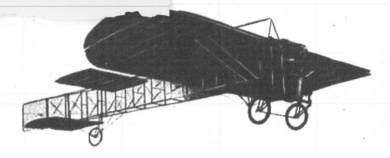

350 1910 MEXICAN REVOLUTION BEGINS

🎓 **BY 1910,** Mexico had been under the dictatorship-like rule of General Porfirio Diaz for more than 30 years. His period of rule (known as the Porfiriato) was characterized by deep political and social unrest, the exploitation of workers and a huge divide between rich and poor.

In 1908, Diaz had given a press interview stating that he wished to promote democracy in Mexico and that he hoped the next Mexican president would be elected democratically. With this in mind, Francisco Madero, a lawyer, ran against Diaz during the 1910 elections. Madero was imprisoned for his troubles and Diaz was declared winner of the elections.

In retaliation, Madero published a document named the Plan of San Luis de Potosi, which called for the people of Mexico to rise in arms against Diaz's authoritarian presidency. As a result, on November 20, 1910, the Mexican Revolution broke out with "Effective Suffrage – No Re-election!" as its battle cry.

After a number of rebel victories across Mexico, Diaz and his vice-president, Ramon Corral resigned from office and the first stage of the Revolution, which would continue for a further nine years, came to an end. The Revolution was to result in over 890,000 Mexican immigrants seeking refuge in the United States.

351 1910 UNION OF SOUTH AFRICA ESTABLISHED

THE TREATY OF VEREENIGING, signed on May 31, 1902, ended the Boer Wars fought between the British Empire on the one side and the South African Republic and the Republic of the Orange Free State on the other. The treaty gave the promise of eventual self-government to the South African Republic (Transvaal) and the Orange Free State, as colonies of the British Empire and under the sovereignty of the British Crown.

With the country now split into four separate self-governing bodies (the Cape Colony had been granted representative government in 1872 and the Natal in 1893), British parliament set up negotiations between the white representatives of the four colonies with the aim of establishing a single Union.

On May 31, 1910, the Union of South Africa (a dominion of the British Empire) was created from Transvaal, Free State, the Cape and Natal. Louis Botha was appointed first prime minister and Jan Smuts his deputy. The new Union governed in the style of Westminster, British and Dutch became the official languages and each colony was responsible for deciding on the voting rights of the blacks population.

Black African opposition was swift and in 1912 the African National Congress was founded to defend their rights and freedoms.

Boer prisoners of war guarded by British soldiers.

352 1911 QING DYNASTY OVERTHROWN

🎓 **BY THE EARLY 1900'S,** the Qing Dynasty was suffering from a weak and unstable central power. When Empress Dowager Cixi and the Guangxu Emperor both died in 1908, the throne was passed to two-year-old Puyi, with his father Prince Chun as regent. Inefficiency and corruption within the Chinese government was rife and civil disorder was commonplace.

Revolutionary groups dissatisfied by the government's conservative policies were founded. One revolutionist, Sun Yat-sen, was responsible for promoting the idea of overthrowing the centuries-old dynastic system in order to replace it with a modern republic. He led a series of failed uprisings and was exiled to the United States.

In October 1911, an accidental bomb explosion led to a police investigation and the discovery of anti-government literature within the New Army. Threatened with execution, the revolutionaries, with the support of the rest of the army, took over the city of Wuchang in what came to be known as

Sun Yat-sen (1866–1925)

the Wuchang Uprising. Within a few weeks the revolt had spread to 15 provinces and brought about the collapse of the Qing Dynasty and almost 2000 years of imperialism. Sun Yat-sen returned from the US and on December 29, 1911 was voted provisional president of the Republic of China.

353 1912 SINKING OF THE TITANIC

🎓 **THE TITANIC** was a passenger steam liner built for the White Star shipping line by Harland and Wolff in Belfast. Weighing over 46,000 tons, she was the largest passenger steamer ever built and, due to specially designed water-tight compartments, was heralded as unsinkable.

Captained by Edward J. Smith, the *Titanic* set sail from Southampton on her maiden voyage on April 10, 1912. After stopping at Cherbourg, France and Queenstown, Ireland to collect additional passengers, the *Titanic* set sail for New York with over 2200 people on board.

On the night of Sunday, April 14, the *Titanic* was in the North Atlantic Ocean, some 400 miles south of Newfoundland, when wireless messages reporting the presence of icebergs in the vicinity of the *Titanic* failed to be relayed to the bridge. Around 11:40 PM the Titanic was struck. A large iceberg that lay directly in the ship's path hit the starboard side and ruptured the hull. At least five compartments filled with water and the bow began to sink, tilting the ship to a vertical position. At 2:20 AM on April 15 the *Titanic* sank. Only 705 of the people on board were rescued.

EASTER
RISING

→ Zimmerman
telegram

BATTLE OF
BRITAIN

WALL ST
CRASH

WINSTON
CHURCHILL

STALINGRAD

Prohibition

ARCHDUKE
FERDINAND

LENIN

The Great Wars

KRISTALLNACHT

PEARL
HARBOR

THE MARNE

HIROSHIMA

treaty of
Versailles

NEW
DEAL!

354 1912–13 BALKAN WARS

🎓 **BY THE EARLY 1900'S,** the Balkan states of Montenegro, Bulgaria, Greece, and Serbia were seeking additional territories within the Turkish Ottoman Empire, and looking to free the remains of the ethnic populations that remained under Ottoman rule.

In 1912, the Balkan states formed an alliance (the Balkan League), and on October 8, 1912, Montenegro declared war on the Ottoman Empire.

The Balkan League formed a combined army of some 645,000 troops, a force substantially larger than the 400,000 troops of the Ottoman's Macedonian, Vardar and Thracian Armies.

The Ottoman armies were spread too thinly to stand up to the Balkan offensive and were soon defeated in Thrace by the Bulgarians. This was followed by a Serbian victory at the Battle of Kumanovo in Macedonia, a Greek victory in Salonika and a Montenegrin victory at the siege of Shkoder in Albania.

The Treaty of London, signed May 30, 1913, ended the First Balkan War and saw the Ottoman Empire lose nearly all of its remaining European territories.

Bulgaria, however, was dissatisfied with the division of territory in Macedonia, and on June 16, 1913 attacked its former allies, Serbia and Greece. The attack was quickly repulsed and the Treaty of Bucharest, signed on August 10, 1913, ended the Second Balkan War with Bulgaria losing much of the territory it had gained during the first war.

Sultan Ahmed Mosque
or Blue Mosque in
Istanbul, Turkey

355 1914 ASSASSINATION OF ARCHDUKE FERDINAND

🎓 **WHEN HIS FATHER,** Carl Ludwig, died in 1896, Archduke Franz Ferdinand became heir presumptive to the throne of Austria-Hungary, which at that time was under the rule of his uncle, Emperor Franz Josef.

On June 28, 1914, Ferdinand and his wife, Sophie Chotek, travelled to Sarajevo, the capital of Bosnia and Herzegovina, on an official visit to inspect the armed forces.

The trip was not without risk, as the move to annex Bosnia and Herzegovina to Austria-Hungary in 1908 had angered Serbian nationalists, who believed the Bosnian territories should be controlled by Serbia. This had led to a series of assassination attempts on Austro-Hungarian officials.

Archduke Franz Ferdinand (1863–1914)

On the day of Ferdinand's visit, a group of assassins, recruited by Danilo Ilic, leader of the Serbian Black Hand terrorist organization, were armed with bombs and a plan to kill the Archduke.

As Ferdinand's motorcade traveled towards the Town Hall in Sarajevo, one of the assassins (Nedeliko Cabrinovic) threw a bomb, which exploded under the car behind Ferdinand, wounding 20 people.

Ferdinand escaped unhurt, but when his car took a wrong turn, 19-year-old Gavrilo Princip stepped out and shot both Ferdinand and his wife at point-blank range. They died almost instantly.

The assassination was to lead to the outbreak of World War I, after Austria-Hungary declared war on Serbia on July 28, 1914.

356 1914 THE BATTLE OF THE MARNE

THE FIRST BATTLE OF THE MARNE was fought on September 5 and 12, 1914 between Germany and the allied forces of France and Britain.

357 FAST FACT...

TAXIS were used to deliver French soldiers to the battlefield of the Marne in September 1914.

During the first month of the World War I, the German army (under Helmuth von Moltke the Younger) was engaged in a sweeping offensive towards Paris, France. This resulted in a number of German victories and the allied army was forced into retreat. By the beginning of September, the French government and thousands of civilians had left Paris.

On September 4, the French army (under Joseph Joffre) and the British Expeditionary Force (under Sir John French) joined forces in order to halt the allied retreat. They began to plan an attack on the German army, which had veered away from Paris and into the Valley of the River Marne, mistakenly exposing their right flank to the allies.

On the morning of September 4, the French Sixth Army met with German troops near the Ourcq River and was initially pushed back. After French reinforcements were brought in, the allies advanced into a gap between the German armies and forced them to retreat northeast, away from Paris.

The allied victory halted the German offensive and marked the beginnings of trench warfare on the Western Front.

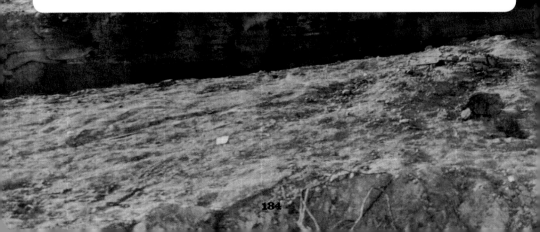

358 FAST FACT...

📖 **HOMING PIGEON** Cher Ami received a Cross of War for delivering 12 vital messages during World War I.

359 1915 SINKING OF THE LUSITANIA

RMS LUSITANIA was a luxury British ocean liner built by John Brown and Company of Clydebank, Scotland. It was mainly used to transport passengers and goods between the United States and Great Britain.

On May 1, 1915, the ship set sail on a course from New York to Liverpool with 1959 passengers on board, 159 of whom were American.

360 FAST FACT...

THE MOST decorated dog of World War I was Stubby the pit bull terrier. He warned his comrades of gas attacks and approaching shellfire.

It was common practice during World War I for each side to be on the look out for enemy vessels. As a consequence, most ships adopted tactics, such as traveling at high speed and zig-zagging to avoid detection. Unfortunately, the *Lusitania* encountered a bank of fog and Captain William Turner slowed the ship, enabling a German U-boat to set its targets.

On May 7 at 1:40 PM, when the *Lusitania* was 14 miles off the southern coast of Ireland, it was struck by a torpedo on its starboard side. A second explosion occurred almost immediately afterwards and within 18 minutes the ship had sunk, killing 1198 of its passengers, including 128 American civilians.

The loss of so many civilian lives enraged America and prompted its entry into the war.

361 1916 THE EASTER RISING, DUBLIN

EVER SINCE BRITAIN had first occupied Ireland in 1169, the call for Home Rule had been the cause of many rebellions and wars, which the Irish had always lost. The Act of Union of 1801, which annexed Ireland to the United Kingdom, and the devastating effects of the Great Potato Famine of 1845–1847, fuelled Irish anger towards British rule.

362 FAST FACT...

MARGARET SANGER was jailed for a month in 1916 for setting up the USA's first birth control clinic.

The formation of the Republican political party Sinn Fein and the 1913 Dublin general strike served as proof of this ever-growing resentment.

In 1916, with World War I underway and Britain engaged in fighting elsewhere, the Irish Republican Brotherhood planned to take advantage and stage an uprising. On Easter Monday (April 24) 1916, members of the Irish Volunteers captured key buildings in Dublin, using the General Post Office on O'Connell Street as headquarters, and the Proclamation of the Irish Republic was declared.

The British sent in thousands of troops and after seven days of fighting and the loss of many British, civilian and rebel lives, the uprising was suppressed.

The Easter Rising was directly responsible for the formation of the Irish parliament (The Dail) in 1919, and the subsequent Irish War of Independence of 1919–21.

363 FAST FACT...

IN 1916, 55% of all the world's cars were Model T Fords.

364 1917 THE BALFOUR DECLARATION

THE BALFOUR DECLARATION was a letter written by Lord Arthur Balfour on November 2, 1917, expressing British support for the establishment of a Jewish homeland in Palestine. It was addressed to Lionel Walter Rothschild, a Zionist activist, and read as follows:

I have much pleasure in conveying to you on behalf of His Majesty's Government, the following declaration of sympathy with Jewish Zionist aspirations which has been submitted to, and approved by, the Cabinet: His Majesty's Government view with favour the establishment in Palestine of a national home for the Jewish people, and will use their best endeavours to facilitate the achievement of this object, it being clearly understood that nothing shall be done which may prejudice the civil and religious rights of existing non-Jewish communities in Palestine, or the rights and political status enjoyed by Jews in any other country.

The wording of the declaration was open to interpretation, but it was formally accepted by allied government representatives at Versailles in 1919 and became the basis for the League of Nations directive regarding Palestine.

Britain was later to backtrack on the Balfour Declaration with the issuing of the White Paper in 1939, which stated that it was no longer British policy to support the creation of a Jewish state. This had a devastating effect on millions of Jews, who were prevented from escaping to Palestine during the Nazi occupation of Europe in World War II.

365 FAST FACT...

DURING WORLD WAR I, the British developed a new secret weapon, code named "water carrier". It was later shortened to "tank".

366 1917 THE OCTOBER REVOLUTION

🎓 **PART OF THE RUSSIAN REVOLUTION** of 1917, the October Revolution (or Red October), took place in Petrograd on October 25, 1917 with a Bolshevik insurrection against the Russian Provisional Government.

367 FAST FACT...

📖 *"Liberty is precious – so precious that it must be rationed."*
– Vladimir Lenin (1870–1924), first ruler of the Soviet Union.

A century of political and civil unrest in Russia culminated in the February Revolution of 1917, when almost the entire city of Petrograd went on strike to demonstrate the extent of their grievances. When Tsar Nicholas II sent in the army to intervene, over 80,000 troops mutinied and joined the demonstrators. The Tsar was forced to abdicate and a Provisional Government was formed by members of the Duma, but the Russian political scene remained in chaos.

At this point, Vladimir Lenin, leading socialist and enemy of the Tsarist state, chose to return to Russia and take advantage of the situation. Promoting his Bolshevik Party with slogans such as, "Peace, Land and Bread," he gradually drew the support of the Russian people. In a planned coup on October 25, the Bolsheviks took control of every key building in Petrograd and eventually the Winter Palace, where members of the Provisional Government were hiding out.

368 FAST FACT...

📖 **THE MOST FEARED** air ace of World War I was Manfred von Richthofen, "The Red Baron," who shot down over 80 Allied planes.

369 FAST FACT...

📖 **CATS** became vital companions for the soldiers serving in the trenches of World War I – they helped keep down the rat population.

On October 26, 1917, power was handed over to the Soviet Council of People's Commissars and Lenin was voted chairman.

370 1917 THE ZIMMERMAN TELEGRAM

FOR THE FIRST three years of World War I, while the European nations were engaged in fighting, the United States had managed to maintain neutrality. It continued to send merchant ships to trade with both Germany and Great Britain and in keeping with his neutral stance, Woodrow Wilson was elected US President for a second term on the back of his "He kept us out of war" slogan.

371 FAST FACT...

📖 DUTCH EXOTIC DANCER

Mata Hari was executed by firing squad in 1917, charged with being a German spy.

However, the sinking of the passenger liner RMS *Lusitania* by a German U-boat in 1915 (*see* p186), and the drowning of 128 American citizens, made it increasingly difficult for Wilson to maintain his neutral position.

In February 1917, Germany broke its pledge to limit submarine warfare and began an unrestricted campaign against all shipping in the Atlantic. Wilson was left with no choice but to sever diplomatic relations with Germany.

In April, the British intercepted and decoded a telegram from the German Foreign Minister, Arthur Zimmerman, to the German ambassador in Mexico. The telegram urged Mexico to seek an alliance with Germany in exchange for US territory. On April 2, 1917, having been unwillingly drawn into unplanned hostilities, Wilson finally instructed Congress to declare war on Germany.

372 FAST FACT...

📖 **A GERMAN U-BOAT** was firing on a British ship in 1917. A truck on the ship's deck was blown into the air and landed on the U-Boat, sinking it.

373 1919 THE TREATY OF VERSAILLES

THE TREATY OF VERSAILLES was one of a series of peace treaties that ended World War I. It dealt specifically with negotiating peace between Germany and the Allied powers. Separate treaties dealt with the other Central powers involved in the war: the St Germain Treaty (Austria), the Trianon Treaty (Hungary), the Neuilly Treaty (Bulgaria), and the Serves Treaty (Turkey).

The Treaty of Versailles was signed on June 28, 1919 during the Paris Peace Conference, which was attended by leaders of 32 states.

Under the main terms of the treaty, Germany was to disarm, surrender all German colonies as League of Nation mandates, limit the German army to 100,000 men and the German Navy to vessels under 100,000 tons with no submarines.

374 FAST FACT...

THE INFLUENZA pandemic (the "Spanish Flu") of 1918–19 was the worst of all time, killing an estimated 25 million people. worldwide.

More importantly, Germany was to accept responsibility for causing the war and was to pay reparations of 132 billion marks (equivalent to 31.4 billion US dollars).

Germany was far from pacified by the heavy-handed terms and signed the treaty under protest. These feelings of resentment were to become a determining factor in igniting World War II.

375 1920 PROHIBITION IN THE UNITED STATES

THE TEMPERANCE MOVEMENT in America had been steadily growing in strength since the seventeenth century. By 1855, the movement – led by strict orthodox religious groups such as the Methodists – had successfully persuaded 13 out of the 33 states to go "dry."

376 FAST FACT...

KING Alexandros I of Greece died in 1920 after being bitten by his pet monkey.

Other groups advocating the prohibition of alcohol, such as the Anti-Saloon League and the Women's Christian Temperance Movement, had become so influential by the end of the Civil War that they were able to convince Congress to pass the Eighteenth Amendment. The amendment stated: *"After one year from the ratification of this article the manufacture, sale, or transportation of intoxicating liquors within, the importation thereof into, or the exportation thereof from the United States and all territory subject to the jurisdiction thereof for beverage purposes is hereby prohibited."*

With a nationwide ban on the sale and consumption of alcohol, the brewing of "moonshine" at home became commonplace and liquor was smuggled from across the borders of Mexico and Canada.

377 FAST FACT...

THE VATICAN CITY became the world's smallest independent nation in 1921. It occupies just 109 acres.

378 FAST FACT...

A MAN ACCUSED of illegally selling alcohol during the Prohibition era had to be acquitted after the jury drank the evidence.

Soon, the illegal manufacture and traffic of alcohol, known as bootlegging, was taken over by organized crime syndicates such as the Mafia. They controlled underground drinking establishments called "speakeasies" and before long mob culture and the violence associated with it had become a major problem.

379 1922 DISCOVERY OF TUTANKHAMEN

🎓 **BORN MAY 9, 1874** in Kensington, London, archeologist Howard Carter worked for the Egyptian Antiquity Service. At the age of 25 he became the first Inspector General of Monuments for Upper Egypt.

380 FAST FACT...

📖 **IN 1924,** the state of Nevada introduced the gas chamber as a more humane form of execution.

Although the Valley of the Kings had been extensively excavated in the past, Carter was convinced that the tomb of a little-known pharaoh, Tutankhamen, was still out there to be discovered.

By 1922, Carter had found little of any significance and his sponsor, Lord Carnarvon, promised him only one more season's worth of funding. Knowing this was his final chance, Carter ordered his men to begin digging at the base of the tomb of Rameses VI.

On November 1, 1922, he unearthed a set of steps that led to one of the world's most important archaeological finds: the lost tomb of Tutankhamen.

381 FAST FACT...

📖 **THE BIGGEST,** most expensive wreath at the 1924 funeral of Chicago gangster Dion O'Banion came from Al Capone, who had ordered O'Banion's murder.

382 FAST FACT...

📖 **THE FRISBEE** was invented in 1925 by American college students tossing and catching the empty circular pie tins of the Frisbie Baking Company.

383 FAST FACT...

📖 **IN 1925,** a dog wandered across the Greek–Bulgarian border. His owner, a Greek soldier, went to retrieve it and was shot. In retaliation, Greece invaded Bulgaria.

384 FAST FACT...

📖 **BLOOD TRANSFUSION** pioneer Dr Alexander Bogdanov began injecting blood into himself from 1925, believing it would give him eternal youth.

Tutankhamen's amazing death mask, discovered in 1922, is made of gold, colored glass and semiprecious stones.

385 1929 THE WALL STREET CRASH

🎓 **AMERICA HAD ENJOYED** a period of major excess during the "Roaring Twenties", which fuelled a false sense of wealth and indestructibility. Banks continued to persuade the middle classes to increase their wealth by investing "on the margin". This meant paying for just 10 per cent of any shares and taking out a loan for the remainder. It was expected that when the shares rose in value, the investor would sell them, pay off their bank loan, and still make a profit.

As share prices rose, it seemed that nobody could lose. With each new profit, investors continued to buy with 10 per cent down payments on ever-larger investments. By October 1929, the national debt stood at six billion dollars. Bankers began to realize that if shares ever began to fall, the results would be disastrous.

386 FAST FACT...

📖 **IN 1926,** a Budapest waiter left a suicide note in the form of a crossword. Police called for help from the public to solve it.

One by one, the banks began to sell and in only a few days, panic had hit Wall Street. By October 29 (Black Tuesday), share prices crashed and 30 million dollars were lost. Banks closed and millions of people were plunged into poverty. It was to be the start of the worst depression in American history.

387 FAST FACT...

📖 **TRANSATLANTIC** phone calls became possible in 1927, but only for the rich. It cost around half the price of a car to talk for just 3 minutes.

388 FAST FACT...

📖 *"Who wants to hear actors talk?"* – Hollywood mogul, Harry M. Warner (1881–1958), when told of the possibility of movies with sound.

389 FAST FACT...

📖 *"Wait a minute! You ain't heard nothin' yet!"* – the first words uttered in *The Jazz Singer*, the first talkie, released in 1927.

390 FAST FACT...

📖 **PEDRO FLORES** reinvented an ancient Filipino weapon as a children's toy when he began selling yo-yos in 1928.

391 1930 THE SALT MARCH

ON MARCH 12, 1930, Mahatma Gandhi, political leader of India during the Indian Independence Movement, led a group of 78 male activists on a 23-day non-violent march from Sabarmati Ashram to the sea coast of Dandi, to protest against the British Salt Tax.

The Salt Tax, imposed on India by the British government, increased the cost of the commodity making it unaffordable for the poor of India. A lack of iodine in their diet resulted in the prevalence of certain diseases. Moreover, it was illegal for workers to collect salt for free from the coasts of India.

Gandhi warned the British Viceroy of his planned protest in a letter which read:

> *If my letter makes no appeal to your heart, on the eleventh day of this month I shall proceed with such co-workers of the Ashram as I can take, to disregard the provisions of the Salt Laws. I regard this tax to be the most iniquitous of all from the poor man's standpoint. As the Independence movement is essentially for the poorest in the land, the beginning will be made with this evil.*

On reaching the coast, Gandhi proceeded to collect salt grains, immediately breaking the law. He was arrested and imprisoned, but his non-violent protest sparked a series of demonstrations across India, which eventually led to India's independence.

392 FAST FACT...

THE FIRST airline stewardess was Ellen Church of Iowa, USA, hired by Boeing Air Transit in 1930.

393 1931 STATUTE OF WESTMINSTER

THE STATUTE OF WESTMINSTER was an Act of British Parliament passed on December 11, 1931, concerning the status of the British dominions of Canada, Australia, New Zealand, South Africa, Ireland and Newfoundland.

Following the peace settlements of World War I and decisions made at the Imperial Conferences of 1926 and 1930, the independence of the British dominions had been recognized. It was declared that the dominions be regarded as:

> *...autonomous communities within the British Empire, equal in status, in no way subordinate one to another in any respect of their domestic or external affairs, though united by a common allegiance to the Crown and freely associated as members of the British Commonwealth of Nations.*

The Statute of Westminster served to clarify this statement by giving formal recognition to the autonomy of the dominions and by establishing their legislative equality. British Parliament could no longer legislate on behalf of the dominions except at their express request. Each dominion would have the right to control its own domestic and foreign affairs and be separately represented in the League of Nations.

The Statute became the founding charter of the British Commonwealth of Nations.

The Houses of Parliament, Westminster

394 1932–36 NEW DEAL

IN 1932, the American public, laid low by the devastating effects of the Depression, elected Franklin Delano Roosevelt to presidency and looked to him to deliver his inaugural promise of a "New Deal" to boost the ravaged economy.

The first "Hundred Days" of the new administration saw a vast array of radical new measures and legislation passed through Congress, all aimed at getting America back on its feet.

The Homeowners Loan Corporation offered funds to those faced with losing their homes, the Federal Deposit Insurance Corporation was set up to protect savings and restore confidence in the banks, and the Civilian Conservation Corps created projects in national forests and parks, which enabled thousands of men to go back to work.

The agricultural industry was given a boost by an injection of federal subsidies, which enabled certain states to build roads, dams and hydroelectric plants, thus bringing more industry and jobs into the region.

395 FAST FACT...

AMERICANS CELEBRATED the ending of Prohibition in 1933 by drinking 1.5 million barrels of beer.

396 FAST FACT...

"The only thing we have to fear is fear itself." – US President Franklin D. Roosevelt, inaugural address (March 4, 1933)

Franklin D. Roosevelt
(1933–1945)

397 1936 THE JARROW MARCH

IN THE AFTERMATH of World War I, Britain's economy was badly hit. During the 1920's and 30's the Great Depression took hold and unemployment levels soared.

The North-East of England was particularly affected, with massive job losses in the predominant coal and ship building industries. With no other form of employment available in the area, miners, shipbuilders and their families suffered extreme hardships and the prospect of starvation.

In the town of Jarrow, Tyne and Wear, the local shipyard (Palmers Shipbuilding and Iron Company Limited) employed 80 per cent of the town's working population until its closure in 1934.

On October 5, 1936, 200 men of Jarrow set off to walk the 280 miles from Jarrow to London in a bid to bring attention to their plight and to lobby parliament for support.Known as the Jarrow Marchers, the men took 22 days to walk the route. With no money or food, the marchers received support, shelter and sustenance from every town they passed through.

On reaching London, the men presented a 12,000-signature petition, but were refused an audience with Prime Minister Stanley Baldwin. The march is remembered as a landmark in the history of the labor movement.

398 1937 THE RAPE OF NANKING

THE RAPE OF NANKING (or the Nanking Massacre) has gone down in history as the single worst atrocity of the Second Sino-Chinese War (1937–1945).

During the war, the Republic of China was pitted against the Empire of Japan in the largest Asian war of the twentieth century. Japan hoped to conquer China both militarily and politically, and to claim its abundance of raw materials.

By 1937, the two powers were engaged in the Battle of Shanghai, one of the largest and bloodiest battles of the war. By November, the Japanese had secured the city and 50,000 of their troops began to advance towards Nanking. On December 13, 1937, Japanese troops entered the city with orders to "kill all captives."

There then followed six weeks of inhuman violence, destruction, deprivation and brutality, with Japanese troops embarking on an orgy of rape, looting, murder and mass executions against Chinese civilians and disarmed Chinese soldiers.

Over 20,000 females, including the elderly, the pregnant and children, were raped and murdered. Much of the city was burned down and the total number of Chinese killed has been estimated at a conservative 300,000.

399 FAST FACT...

A RADIO BROADCAST of H. G. Wells's *War of the Worlds* caused mass panic in 1938, when listeners mistook it for news of a real Martian invasion.

To this day, many Japanese deny the atrocity ever took place and the Japanese government has refused to apologize.

Nanjing, China

400 1938 THE MUNICH AGREEMENT

🎓 **FOLLOWING THE RE-DELINEATION** of the European map in the aftermath of World War I, some three million Germans came to be living in an area of Czechoslovakia known as the Sudetenland.

After Adolf Hitler came to power in Germany, he was determined to bring the Sudeten Germans into the Reich and began to mobilize his army along the Czech border.

In an attempt to avert a situation that could lead to full-scale war, the British Prime Minister Neville Chamberlain (also representing the French government)

Adolf Hitler (1889–1945)

met with Hitler at Hitler's private home in Berchtesgaden, Germany, to discuss the matter. Hitler proved forceful, and gave Britain, and France a deadline of September 28, 1938, to accept his intention of taking Sudetenland or risk a German invasion of the whole of Czechoslovakia.

401 FAST FACT...

📖 *"I believe it is peace for our time."* – British prime minister Neville Chamberlain, on returning from talks with Adolf Hitler, September 1938.

At the suggestion of Italy's Mussolini, the four powers of Germany, France, Britain and Italy met at a crisis-avoiding conference in Munich on September 29, 1938. Seeing no other way of avoiding war, and having secured Hitler's promise to make no further territorial demands, Britain and France eventually agreed to Hitler's claim on the Sudetenland. The region was handed over to Germany with the signing of the Munich Agreement.

Only six months later, in March 1939, Hitler broke the agreement by seizing the rest of Czechoslovakia.

402 1938 KRISTALLNACHT

FOLLOWING THE FORCED expulsion of over 15,000 Jews from their homes in Germany in October 1938, Herschel Grynszpan, a young Jew living in Paris after the deportation, shot a German Embassy member of staff in revenge for the treatment of his family.

Hitler and Nazi Propaganda Minister Joseph Goebbels seized on the incident to organise a mass co-ordinated attack on Jews, their properties and businesses. Orders to the Gestapo included the instructions, "Actions against Jews, especially against their synagogues, will take place throughout the Reich shortly."

On the night of November 9, 1938, later known as Kristallnacht (or The Night of Broken Glass), police stood by as Nazi stormtroopers, and civilians roused to anger by antisemitic propaganda, destroyed Jewish homes, schools, hospitals, and shops. Across Germany and Austria, over 7500 Jewish businesses were destroyed, 267 synagogues burnt down, and countless Jews beaten and brutalized – 91 were killed. Over 25,000 Jewish men were seized and sent to concentration camps.

Kristallnacht shocked the world and added to Germany's isolation, but the events of that night proved to be only the first step in Hitler's Final Solution.

403 FAST FACT...

"Political power grows out of the barrel of a gun." – Mao Tse-tung (1893–1976)

🎓 **FOLLOWING THE GERMAN** invasion of Czechoslovakia in March 1939, Adolf Hitler set his sights on Poland.

France had a military agreement in place with Poland dating from 1921, and on March 31, 1939, after Germany had flouted the Munich Agreement, Britain also pledged to support Poland in the event of an invasion.

True to his intent, at dawn on September 1, 1939, Hitler sent a massive German army across the border of Poland in what became known as the Blitzkrieg – a highly effective "lightning war" involving fast-moving tanks, motorized infantry, and air bombers.

On the morning of September 3, 1939, the British ambassador to Germany, Sir Neville Henderson, delivered an ultimatum to Hitler, declaring that if plans to withdraw German troops from Poland were not issued by 11 AM, then a state of war would exist between Britain and Germany. The French presented an ultimatum at 12:30 PM with a deadline of 5 PM.

At 11:15 AM, with no German response forthcoming, British Prime Minister Neville Chamberlain announced to the British public, via radio, that Britain was now at war with Germany. France declared war on Germany later the same day.

The Allied forces were caught unawares by the German army's Blitzkrieg tactics, expecting battles to develop slowly. The speed with which German forces spread across Europe, using tanks and combat aircraft, showed how outdated the Allied strategy had become.

405 1940 THE BATTLE OF BRITAIN

THE BATTLE OF BRITAIN was a major aerial campaign fought between the German Air Force (the *Luftwaffe*), and the British Royal Air Force (RAF) during World War II. It is the only battle ever to be fought entirely in the air.

406 FAST FACT...

"I HAVE nothing to offer but blood, toil, tears and sweat."
– Winston Churchill, upon taking over as prime minister, May 1940.

407 FAST FACT...

THE BATTLE OF BRITAIN involved over 6000 German and British planes.

In 1940, Hitler released his plans for an invasion of Great Britain by sea, dubbed Operation Sea Lion. Gaining control of the English Channel was a crucial part of the plan, but Germany would have to first control the skies to prevent the British RAF from destroying German vessels.

On July 10, 1940, the *Luftwaffe* launched its first attack on British ships in the Channel and on Channel ports. By August, the *Luftwaffe* were targeting airfields, radar stations, harbors, and aircraft factories.

With the aim of destroying the RAF on the ground and in the air, the *Luftwaffe* intensified its raids, targeting in particular the airfields of 11 Group. Night raids were introduced to prevent repairs to damaged RAF aircraft being carried out overnight.

When a civilian area of London was accidentally bombed, the British retaliated with a bombing raid over Berlin. An incensed Hitler changed tactics and switched to attacking British civilian targets in what came to be known as the Blitz.

This change in tactics gave the RAF chance to reassemble its defences and the *Luftwaffe* began to experience heavy losses. By autumn, Hitler realized that the RAF could not be defeated. He turned his attention to Russia and cancelled Operation Sea Lion.

408 FAST FACT...

THE FIRST Allied air raid on Germany killed the only elephant in Berlin Zoo.

409 1941 PEARL HARBOR

👨‍🎓 **SINCE THE 1920'S,** relations between the United States and Japan had been deteriorating rapidly. Tensions were further heightened in 1937, when Japan declared war on China and later formed the Tripartite Pact with Italy and Germany.

410 FAST FACT...

📖 **THE ISLAND** of Jersey was the only part of Britain to be occupied by Nazi Germany during World War II.

In a move designed to deter Japanese hostilities, President Roosevelt issued an embargo on exports of oil and raw materials to Japan and transferred the US Pacific Fleet from San Diego to Pearl Harbor, Hawaii. Far from acting as a deterrent, this action was seen as a threat and prompted Japan into launching a full-scale attack against America.

On the morning of December 7, 1941, over 300 Japanese aircraft flew into Pearl Harbor and destroyed or damaged a vast proportion of the US Pacific Fleet. The attack killed 2400 American personnel and wounded over 1200.

America could no longer keep out of World War II. The following day, a formal declaration of war was made against Japan, with Roosevelt declaring, *"No matter how long it may take us to overcome this premeditated invasion, the American people, in their righteous might, will win through to absolute victory."*

411 FAST FACT...

📖 **THE YOUNGEST** US serviceman to fight in World War II was just 12 years old. He lied about his age so he could join up.

412 1942 FIRST SUSTAINED NUCLEAR CHAIN REACTION

🎓 **THE 1930'S** was a decade of great scientific advancement, particularly in the field of nuclear physics. Leading the way was Italian-born American physicist Enrico Fermi. He was awarded the Nobel Prize for Physics in 1938 for his, "demonstrations of the existence of new radioactive elements produced by neutron irradiation." He moved to New York not long after to work at Columbia University, where he collaborated with a number of other scientists on the first nuclear fission experiment in the United States.

In 1939, Albert Einstein and Austro-Hungarian physicist Leo Szilard composed a letter to President Roosevelt warning that Nazi Germany was possibly building an atomic bomb and the nuclear race was initiated. Fermi relocated to Chicago and, with money from the US government, helped develop the first nuclear reactor (Chicago Pile-1) as part of the Manhattan Project.

On December 2, 1942, at 3:25 PM, under the supervision of Fermi, Chicago Pile-1 went critical – that is to say, the world's first sustained nuclear chain reaction was achieved. This landmark moment paved the way for the building of the atomic bombs used at Hiroshima and Nagasaki.

Albert Einstein
(1879–1955)

413 1942–43 THE BATTLE OF STALINGRAD

THE BATTLE OF STALINGRAD was fought during the winter of 1942–43 between the Russian Red Army and the German 6th Army, assisted by the 4th Panzer army, for the control of the Russian city of Stalingrad.

The capture of Stalingrad was important to Germany, allowing her to secure the oil fields of Caucasus, cutting off Russia's fuel supply. As the city bore the name of the Russian leader, Stalin, its capture would also serve as a massive propaganda coup.

414 FAST FACT...

DURING the siege of Leningrad, Russia, in 1941–2, the city's starving population resorted to eating rats, pets, and even tree bark.

At the end of August 1942, the German 6th Army advanced towards Stalingrad. Supported by the *Luftwaffe*, the Germans bombed the city heavily, reducing much of it to rubble. The Red Army stood its ground, and the battle became one of fierce hand to hand combat. The Germans, who were used to the swift, devastating effects of their Blitzkrieg tactics, were disorientated.

In November, the Red Army launched a two-pronged attack on the 6th Army's flanks, the success of which saw the Germans effectively trapped in the city. A harsh Russian winter further weakened the 6th Army and by February, the bloodiest battle of World War II finally came to an end with almost two million casualties. The German defeat at Stalingrad was a major turning point in the war, and one from which the weakened German forces never fully recovered.

415 FAST FACT...

DURING World War II, the Russian army used dogs strapped with explosives to blow up German tanks.

416 1942 OPERATION TORCH

OPERATION TORCH was a combined British-American invasion of Vichy French-controlled North Africa that occurred November 8–12, 1942.

Russia had pressed the Allies to open up a new western front in the war against Germany, diverting the German army away from Russia and easing the pressure on Russian troops.

The Americans favored landing in occupied Europe, but were persuaded by the British that a successful North African operation would clear the region and the Mediterranean Sea of the Axis powers, and would set the stage for an allied invasion of southern Europe the following year.

417 FAST FACT...

THE FIRST computer bug was a real bug – a moth crawled inside an early naval computer in 1943, causing it to malfunction.

On November 8, 1942, the Allies landed three task forces on the North African coast. The Western Task Force landed at Safi, near Casablanca, the Central Task Force at Oran and the Eastern Task Force at Algiers. After some minor resistance from the French, the Western Task Force, under Major-General George Patton, took control of Casablanca on November 10. The other two Task Forces achieved similar success, with French forces in Oran and Algiers surrendering within a day.

The Allies, now free to advance on Tunisia, met with the German Afrika Korps, under Commander Rommel (in retreat after being defeated at El Alamein). Heavy fighting occurred at Faid Pass and at the Kasserine Pass, but by May 13, 1943, the Axis forces in Tunisia had surrendered.

418 FAST FACT...

IN 1943, the US armed forces became the world's largest ice cream manufacturer, producing 80 million gallons per year for US troops.

THE TERM "UNITED NATIONS" was first coined by US President Roosevelt when referring to the union of the Allied nations in their fight against the Axis powers during World War II.

Wanting to keep this union intact and maintain peace after the war ended, 26 countries signed The Declaration of United Nations on January 1, 1942.

In October 1943, in Moscow, the formalization of the United Nations into an international peace-keeping organization was first discussed at a conference of foreign ministers looking to replace the beleaguered League of Nations.

Franklin D. Roosevelt (left) and Winston Churchill (right) in 1943.

With this in mind, the Dumbarton Oaks Conference, held in Washington DC from August to October 1944, was organized specifically for representatives of China, the United Kingdom, the Soviet Union, and the United States to discuss the details of what was to become the new world body of the United Nations.

Issues addressed included the proposed structure of the Security Council, its use of the power of veto, and the Soviet Union's insistence on separate membership for 16 of its republics.

From April to June 1945, representatives of 50 nations that had been at war with Germany met in San Francisco to draft and adopt the first United Nations Charter. This was ratified in London at the first session of the General Assembly of the United Nations on October 24, 1945.

420 1944–1945 THE BATTLE OF THE BULGE

THE BATTLE OF THE BULGE (or the Ardennes Offensive), was Hitler's last offensive of World War II and took place from December 16, 1944 to January 25, 1945.

Allied forces had landed in Normandy, France on July 6, 1944 (D-Day) to begin the liberation of Europe. German forces, already split in two by fighting on the eastern and western fronts, lacked weapons and morale and were gradually being driven back through France.

Unable to contemplate defeat, Hitler knew his only option was to launch an offensive. Amid great secrecy, Operation "Watch on the Rhine" was launched on December 16, 1944, in the Ardennes Forest, an area left unprotected by the Allies.

The Allies were taken by surprise and within three days the Germans had created a "bulge" in the Allied front line. On December 17, an arm of the German forces known as Kampfgruppe Peiper, shot dead around 85 American prisoners of war. The Malmedy Massacre, as it has become known, was never explained.

Bad weather conditions initially hampered the Allies' defensive efforts, but by the end of December, with improved conditions, they were able to strike back with air attacks and bombing raids. By the end of January, the Germans had suffered crushing losses, both in the air and on the ground. The remaining German forces were pushed back to the Siegfried Line and a major turning point in the war was reached.

421 FAST FACT...

THE FIRST US soldier to jump from his boat during the Anzio landings in 1944 was 6 feet 6 inches-tall James Arness – chosen to test the depth of the water.

The A-Bomb Dome in Hiroshima, Japan. The building was preserved after the bombing and is now part of the Hiroshima Peace Memorial Park.

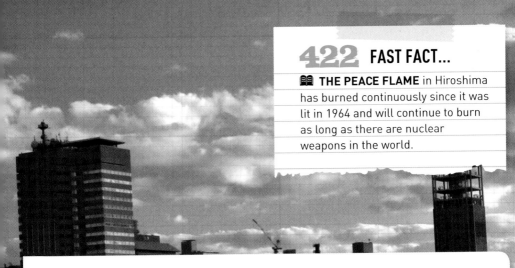

422 FAST FACT...

📖 **THE PEACE FLAME** in Hiroshima has burned continuously since it was lit in 1964 and will continue to burn as long as there are nuclear weapons in the world.

423 1945 ATOMIC BOMBING OF JAPAN

🎓 **PRESIDENT HARRY S. TRUMAN** was notified of the development of the "most terrible weapon ever known in human history" less than two weeks into his presidency. When Japan dismissed America's attempts to negotiate peace during the summer of 1945, Truman authorized the use of the world's first atomic bombs.

On August 6, 1945, a B-29 bomber took off from Tinian Island in the South Pacific carrying "Little Boy," a 10-foot uranium-235 atomic bomb. At 8:15 AM local time, it flew over the Japanese city of Hiroshima and dropped "Little Boy." The bomb exploded 1900 feet over the city, decimating two-thirds of Hiroshima and instantly killing over 70,000 civilians. A further 70,000 people died within five years from radiation poisoning.

Three days later, a second B-29 bomber flew from Tinian Island towards its target of Kokura. Heavy cloud coverage prevented the pilot from carrying out his mission and the plane was diverted to its second target of Nagasaki. At 11.02 AM local time, the bomber dropped a plutonium-239 atomic bomb named "Fat Boy," which exploded 1650 feet above the city. Over 70,000 civilians were killed and 40 per cent of Nagasaki was destroyed.

On August 15, 1945 Japan's Emperor, Hirohito, announced his surrender to the Allies and signed The Instrument of Surrender on September 2. World War II had finally come to an end.

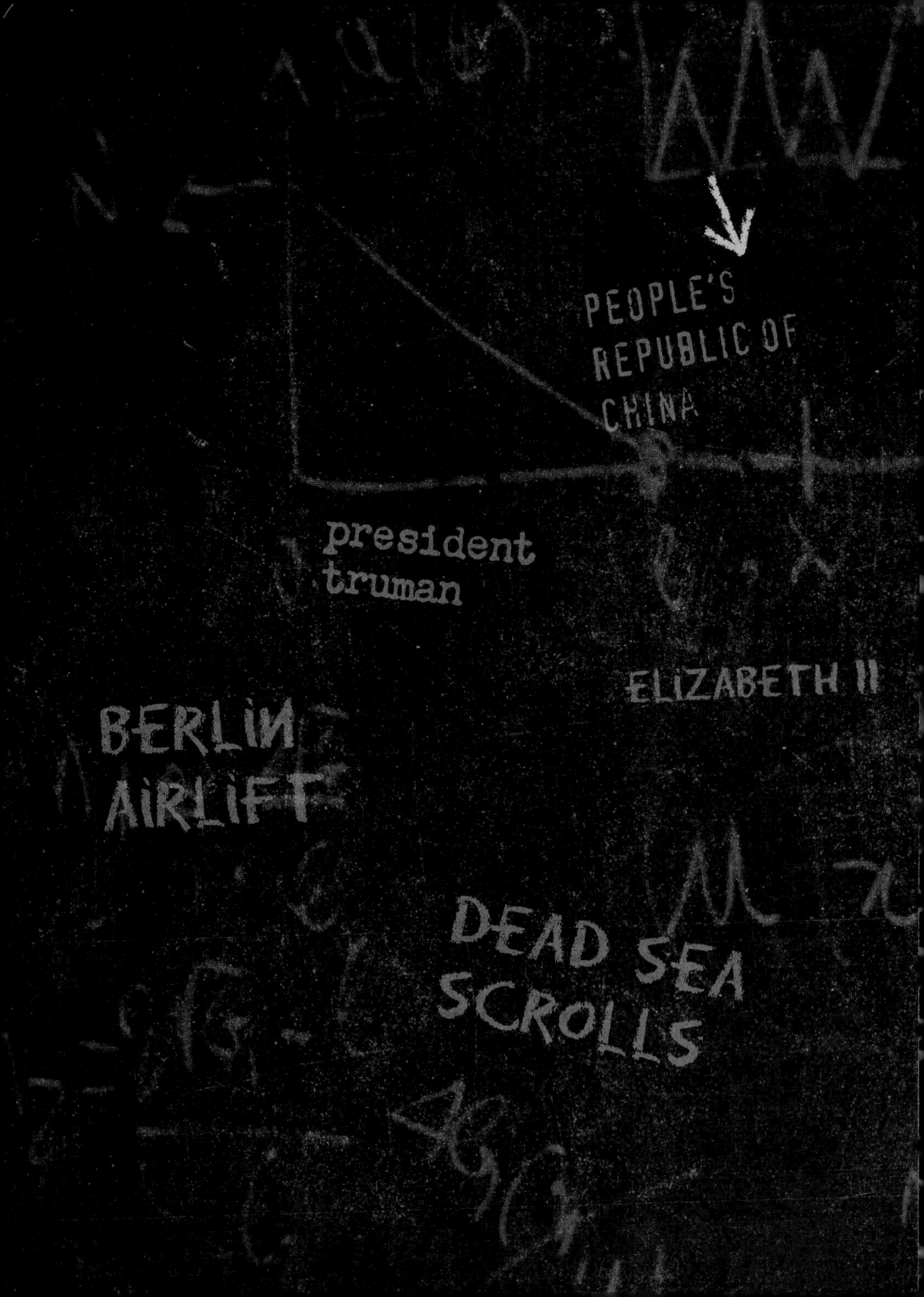

PEOPLE'S
REPUBLIC OF
CHINA

president
truman

ELIZABETH II

BERLIN
AIRLIFT

DEAD SEA
SCROLLS

REGENERATION

KOREAN WAR

Recovery

50

MAO

WARSAW PACT

AL CAPONE

APARTHEID

marshall plan

STALIN

424 1947–56 DEAD SEA SCROLLS

THE DEAD SEA SCROLLS are a collection of around 900 ancient scrolls and manuscripts, which were discovered between 1947–56 in 11 caves that are scattered about the hills above the northwest shore of the Dead Sea (an area now known as the West Bank, in the Palestinian territories of Western Asia).

The scrolls are written in Hebrew, Aramaic, and Greek, and are believed to have been scribed by a sectarian Jewish tribe from Qumran. Dating from around 170 BC to the first century AD, the library of documents represents the greatest manuscript find of the twentieth century.

The scrolls, many of which had broken into tiny fragments, contain the oldest known surviving copies of the Hebrew Bible.

The discovery of Old Testament texts, psalms and many other works, including previously unknown Biblical stories, has served to illuminate the diversity of Jewish beliefs at the time.

Divided into three groups (Biblical, Apocryphal, and Sectarian manuscripts) the scrolls are made of animal skin, papyrus, and one of copper. The longest scroll found (the Temple Scroll) measures around 26 feet in length.

425 FAST FACT...

PIONEERING cosmetic surgeon Archibald McIndoe treated hundreds of young soldiers who had suffered facial burns during World War II.

426 FAST FACT...

FRENCH ENGINEER Louis Reard launched the bikini in July 1946, named after Bikini Atoll, the site of atomic weapons tests.

427 1947 THE MARSHALL PLAN

🎓 **ON MARCH 12, 1942**, President Truman proposed a reversal of United States foreign policy from a non-intervention stance to possible military, political, and economical intervention in foreign conflicts. This developed into the Truman Doctrine, which pledged support for *"free peoples who are resisting attempted subjugation by armed minorities or by outside pressures."*

428 FAST FACT...

📖 *"People will soon get tired of staring at a plywood box every night."*
– Movie producer Darryl F Zanuck in 1946, speaking about television.

On March 5, 1947, in a speech at Harvard University, Secretary of State George C. Marshall went one step further, with his planned program of American aid to help rebuild a Europe devastated by the effects of World War II. In an effort to stabilize the political and economical situation in Europe and to diminish the influence of communism, Marshall stated, *"It is logical that the United States should do whatever it is able to do to assist in the return of normal economic health in the world, without which there can be no political stability and no assured peace. Our policy is directed not against any country or doctrine but against hunger, poverty, desperation, and chaos."*

In the three years of its existence, the European Recovery Program or the Marshall Plan, donated over $12.5 billon towards this cause.

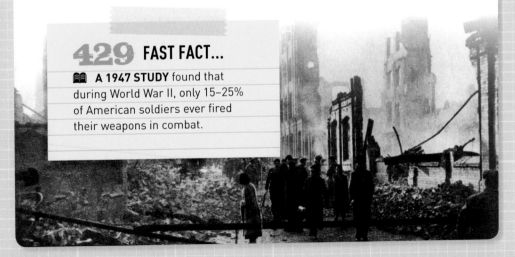

429 FAST FACT...

📖 **A 1947 STUDY** found that during World War II, only 15–25% of American soldiers ever fired their weapons in combat.

430 1948–49 THE BERLIN AIRLIFT

📖 **POST-WAR BERLIN** – situated in the heart of Soviet-controlled eastern Germany – was split into four zones; three controlled by the western allies and the fourth by the Soviet Union.

By March 1948, Stalin had bled East Germany and East Berlin dry in his determination to make Germany pay for war damages. Meanwhile, the western-controlled zones of Berlin had united into a single zone to create West Berlin, an independent capitalist state. A new currency (the Deutsche Mark) was introduced by the western allies. Stalin refused to recognize either the currency or the creation of West Berlin, and in an effort to halt a possible German economic resurgence, he ordered the blockading of all access, and supply of food and fuel to the city, thereby initiating what was to become the first crisis of the Cold War.

Josef Stalin (1878–1953)

Determined to not let Stalin gain control of West Berlin, US President Truman organised an emergency airlift to supply the blockaded city with food and fuel. Over a 10-month period, 2,245,315 tons of food and supplies were delivered to the city. The operation was a resounding success and on May 11, 1949, an embarrassed Stalin was forced to lift the Berlin Blockade, paving the way for the establishment of the separate states of East and West Berlin.

431 FAST FACT...

📖 **GANGSTER AL CAPONE** died in 1947. On his business card he described himself as a used furniture dealer.

432 FAST FACT...

📖 **IN 1947**, US pilot Chuck Yeager became the first human to travel faster than the speed of sound.

433 1949–50 CREATION OF PEOPLE'S REPUBLIC OF CHINA

🎓 **BORN TO A PEASANT FAMILY** in Chaochan, China in 1893, Mao Zedong was drawn to Marxism as a young man. In 1921, he became a founding member of the Chinese Communist Party. Instructed by the Soviet Comintern, Mao and fellow CCP members joined China's National People's Party (the Kuomintang). Mao worked as a political organizer in Shanghai until the death of Sun Yat-sen, the Kuomintang leader, and the subsequent expulsion of communists from the party by its new leader, Chiang Kai-Shek. This encouraged Mao and other survivors of the purge to form the Jiangxi Soviet, an independent government based in the Jiangxi province in south eastern China.

Forced to flee, following attacks from the Kuomintang, Mao led 80,000 troops of the Red Army of China on a legendary 6000-mile march to the north to establish a new communist base. Only a tenth of the troops survived the journey.

During the Japanese invasion of China in 1937, Chiang Kai-Shek was forced to form a united front with Mao's communist forces in order to repel the invasion. With the Japanese surrender at the end of the World War II, Mao and his army turned their attention back to the Kuomintang and in 1949, Mao took control of China and announced the creation of the People's Republic of China.

434 FAST FACT...

📖 **SIMON**, a ship's cat on HMS *Amethyst* in 1949, performed so well under fire that he was awarded the Animal VC and the rank of "Able Seacat."

在需要夺权的那些地方和单位，必须
实行革命的"三结合"的方针，建立一个革
命的、有代表性的、有无产阶级权威的临
时权力机构。这个权力机构的名称，叫革
命委员会好。　　　　　　毛泽东

435 1949 APARTHEID INTRODUCED TO SOUTH AFRICA

THE LEGAL SYSTEM OF APARTHEID (Afrikaans for "separateness")
was introduced to South Africa after the National Party came to power in 1948.
Apartheid laws formalized racial segregation and racial hatred.

The National Party was founded by J.B.M. Hertzog in 1914 in protest against
the anglicising policies of Louis Botha's South African Party. After forming a
coalition with the Labour Party in 1924, Hertzog became prime minister.
In 1930, he doubled white political power by granting the vote to white women,
thus undermining the vote of mixed white and non-white South Africans.

From 1933–39, Hertzog merged with the South African Party to form the United
Party. However, staunch members of the original National Party continued to
garner support and, after re-organizing into the Reunited National Party in
1939, they eventually triumphed in the 1948 elections and began to implement
a program of apartheid by enacting laws such as the Prohibition of Mixed
Marriages Act, which prohibited marriage between white people and those of
other races. The Group Areas Act forced different races to live in separated
residential areas and the Reservation of Separate Amenities Act forced
segregation in public buildings and on public transport.

Cape Town,
South Africa

436 1950 THE KOREAN WAR

WHEN WORLD WAR II came to an end in August 1945, the Japanese-occupied Korean Peninsula was divided along the thirty-eighth parallel; the north being influenced by the Soviet Union and the south receiving the support of the United States. Intended as a temporary measure until an independent Korean government could be installed, the division was disputed by the Soviets, who wanted to claim North Korea as a communist territory. When the Russian Red Army moved to fortify the thirty-eighth parallel, the US intervened and ruled that an election should be held, with the resulting government being protected by a United Nations security force.

Resistance from North Korea resulted in a split election and the formation of the Republic of Korea and its rival in the north, the People's Democratic Republic of Korea.

With the US determined to contain the spread of communism, tensions escalated until on June 25, 1950, the North Korean People's Army invaded South Korea and took control of the capital city of Seoul.

A bloody war ensued, with America calling upon the assistance of the United Nations and its member states, and with the Soviet Union forming an alliance with communist China.

Months of heavy fighting, mostly along the thirty-eighth parallel, finally reached stalemate, with peace talks beginning at the end of June 1951. It was not until April 1953 that a cease-fire was agreed, and an armistice was eventually signed on July 27, 1953. Despite the loss of nearly two million lives, North and South Korea remained divided.

437 FAST FACT...

IN 1952, George Jorgensen, a former US army GI, became the first person to undergo gender reassignment surgery. He became a woman called Christina.

438 FAST FACT...

WITCHCRAFT laws were finally lifted in Britain in 1951.

439 1955 WARSAW PACT

THE WARSAW PACT (or the Warsaw Treaty of Friendship, Cooperation and Mutual Assistance) was signed in Warsaw on May 14, 1955 at the initiation of the Soviet Union. Created in response to the decision of the Paris Pacts of 1954 to allow West Germany to join NATO (which the Soviets saw as a direct threat to the reunification of Germany and the security of the Eastern bloc countries), the pact was signed by the USSR, Poland, East Germany, Czechoslovakia, Hungary, Romania, Bulgaria, and Albania. The only eastern bloc country to be excluded was Yugoslavia, which had been expelled from the Communist Information Agency in 1948 for failing to acknowledge Soviet supremacy.

According to the premier of the Soviet Union, Nikolai Bulganin, the pact was based upon the, *"Leninist principle of peaceful co-operation between democratic nations,"* and was to adhere to the United Nations Charter.

The armies of all eight countries were unified under the command of Marshal Ivan Stepanovich Konev and a Red Army force was stationed in each member state. This allowed the Soviet Union to crush nationalist rebellions such as the 1956 Hungarian and 1968 Czechoslovakian uprisings that were to follow.

Warsaw Old
Town, Poland

440 FAST FACT...

CELLIST AMBROSE GAUNTLETT, chosen to play at Queen Elizabeth II's coronation in 1953, smuggled a camera into Westminster Abbey, becoming the first paparazzo.

CUBAN
MISSILE
CRISIS

WORLD WIDE
WEB

BARACK
OBAMA

MOON
LANDING   9/11

NELSON MANDELA

MARTIN
LUTHER
KING

Pope John
Paul II.

SPACE RACE

J.F.K

Modern History

BERLIN WALL

CIVIL RIGHTS

WATERGATE

KHMER ROUGE

ARAB SPRING

VIETNAM WAR

441 1956 THE HUNGARIAN REVOLUTION

THE HUNGARIAN REVOLUTION of October 23–November 10, 1956 was a public revolt against Soviet-imposed policies.

Hungary had been under Soviet rule since 1945. When Stalin died in 1953, the people of Hungary hoped they would be freed from the "iron grip" of Russia. But when the new Russian leader, Khrushchev, came to power, his only concessions extended to his denouncement of Stalin's policies and the removal of the Hungarian leader, Rakosi (originally placed in office by Stalin) from power.

442 FAST FACT...

THE CAVERN CLUB in Liverpool, England opened in 1957. After their first performance there in 1961, *The Beatles* would become the club's signature act.

This, combined with a bad harvest, fuel shortages, and general unrest, was enough to push students and workers onto the streets of Budapest on October 23, 1956, to demand more freedom, food, and the removal of Soviet control. Violence erupted across the city, Stalin's statue was smashed, and the State Security Police were attacked.

The government quickly fell and Hungarian politician Imre Nagy was installed as prime minister. Soviet troops withdrew from the city and on October 29, the new government announced Hungary's withdrawal from the Warsaw Pact and its intentions to introduce democracy and freedom of speech.

The Soviets retaliated and on November 4, Russian tanks advanced on Budapest. By November 10, the revolution had been crushed and a new Soviet-installed government was in place.

443 FAST FACT...

WHEN ELVIS PRESLEY appeared on TV in 1957, the producers were so concerned that his hip swaying might offend viewers that they only showed him from the waist up.

The Hungarian
Parliament, Budapest

444 1956 EGYPT NATIONALIZES SUEZ CANAL

ON JULY 26, 1956, Egyptian President Gamal Abdel Nasser announced the nationalization of the British and French-controlled Suez Canal Company. The intention was to charge tolls in order to finance the building of the Aswan Dam across the River Nile. The United States and Western powers had previously withdrawn offers to help fund the project, amid concerns over Egypt's developing relationship with the Soviet Union.

The Suez Canal Company had always been legally Egyptian, but was not due to revert to the Egyptian Government until November 1968, due to a 99-year concession that had been granted in 1869.

445 FAST FACT...

THE BARBIE DOLL, released in 1959, was named after Barbara, the daughter of the doll's creator, Ruth Handler.

The nationalization of the canal shocked the British and French governments, and when diplomatic talks with Egypt failed to reach a satisfactory compromise, Britain and France joined forces with Egypt's long term-enemy, Israel, to take over the canal and topple Nasser.

On October 29, 1956, the joint British, French and Israeli armies marched on the canal and took control of the Suez region. The crisis escalated and Nasser responded by sinking all 40 ships present in the canal at the time, blocking the passage for all shipping.

The US and the rest of the world condemned the invasion and by early 1957, Britain and France had been persuaded to back down. Israel withdrew in March. The canal reverted to Egyptian control under the agreement that it be open for free passage to all nations.

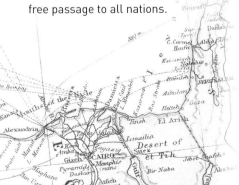

446 FAST FACT...

AT THE HEIGHT of the Cold War in the 1950's and 1960's, up to a third of East Berliners were spying on the rest of the population.

447 1957 A DOG CALLED LAIKA

DURING THE MID-TO-LATE twentieth century, America and the USSR competed in what was known as the "Space Race". Each nation wanted to achieve firsts in the sphere of space exploration, and both conducted pioneering experiments in the hope of launching artificial satellites, enabling human space flight, and sending manned voyages to the moon.

In order to ascertain the suitability of space flight for humans, animals were used to test spacesuits and un-pressurised space capsule cabins.

On October 4, 1957, the Soviets launched the world's first artificial satellite, *Sputnik 1*, into orbit. To demonstrate their belief that living organisms from Earth could survive in space, on November 3, 1957, they sent a live dog named Laika into orbit aboard the world's second artificial satellite, *Sputnik 2*.

Laika was a three-year-old stray Siberian husky. She was attached to a life support system within the space capsule, with access to food and water.

A few days into the voyage, as expected, the life support batteries died and Laika passed away in space (however, recent evidence now suggests that Laika died from panic and over-heating only a few hours into the mission).

Sputnik 2 circled the earth 2570 times before burning up as it re-entered the atmosphere on April 4, 1958. Laika's journey paved the way for human spaceflight and a monument in her honor was erected in Moscow.

448 FAST FACT...

IN THE 1960'S, the USA and the Soviet Union recruited teams of dolphins to locate underwater mines and blow up enemy ships and submarines.

449 1961 THE BAY OF PIGS

WHEN FIDEL CASTRO took control of Cuba in 1959, the close proximity of a communist stronghold unnerved the United States government, which was already dealing with the ongoing tensions of the Cold War.

Plans to invade Cuba had begun under President Eisenhower, but approval for the invasion was not given until John F. Kennedy took office in January 1961.

450 FAST FACT...

THE WORLD'S FIRST computer game, Spacewar, was created by a couple of students in 1961.

451 FAST FACT...

ON NOVEMBER 9, 1965, there was a 9-hour blackout across north-eastern USA and southern Canada. Nine months later there was a surge in the birth rate.

Rather than use US troops, Cuban exiles were trained and equipped to be dropped in the Bay of Pigs, Cuba, in the hope they would incite an anti-Castro revolt.

On April 17, 1961, around 1300 exiles were landed at the Bay of Pigs. A pre-emptive US air strike had already proved less than effective, and it soon became clear that due to Castro's popularity, the exiles were not going to find the hoped-for support from the local Cuban population. The invasion was a disaster. Fearing a Soviet retaliation, Kennedy ordered the US navy and the air force to pull out, leaving the exiles to be either captured or killed.

The failed invasion seriously embarrassed the Kennedy administration and served only to fuel pro-communist feelings in Cuba.

452 FAST FACT...

THE FOOTBALL WAR between El Salvador and Honduras was sparked by a fight between rival fans after a match in July 1969.

453 1961 BUILDING OF THE BERLIN WALL

BETWEEN 1949 AND 1961, 2.7 million people crossed from the German Democratic Republic and East Berlin into the American, British, and French-occupied West Berlin. This mass migration prompted the leaders of the East German Communist Party (SED) to take action, in order to contain the people and halt the threatened economic and social collapse.

In the early hours of August 13, 1961, a temporary barbed wire barrier was erected across the city, dividing streets, squares and public areas and effectively imprisoning over 17 million people. Overnight, families and friends were separated and for many, access to places of employment was cut off.

In a speech to the House of Representatives later the same evening, the Governing Mayor of West Berlin, Willy Brandt, announced that *"The Berlin Senate publicly condemns the illegal and inhuman measures being taken by those who are dividing Germany, oppressing East Berlin, and threatening West Berlin."*

In the weeks that followed, the barbed wire was replaced by concrete blocks. The resulting wall, built by East Berlin construction workers, was almost 13 feet high and was interspersed with watchtowers manned by armed border guards.

Between 1961 and the dismantling of the wall in 1989, over 100,000 East Berliners tried to escape into West Berlin. At least 140 of them died in the attempt.

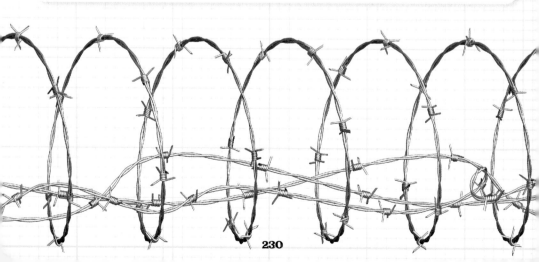

🎓 **THE ATTEMPTED US-BACKED INVASION** of the Bay of Pigs in 1961 drove the Cuban Communists to turn to the Soviet Union for support. Soviet president Khrushchev was happy to oblige as the USSR was keen to build missile bases in Cuba, close enough to be within firing range of the United States mainland. Furthermore, Khrushchev had been encouraged by America's failure to take military action to support the invading Cuban rebels, something widely regarded in the USSR as evidence of Kennedy's weakness.

In 1962, when US intelligence detected Soviet missile bases being built in Cuba, Kennedy ordered a full naval blockade and demanded the removal of all Soviet arms and bases from Cuba.

Khrushchev ignored US demands and sent Soviet battleships to advance on Cuba. The stand-off lasted a tense 13 days, during which time talk of nuclear warfare prompted Kennedy to announce that that the US would *"regard any nuclear missile launched from Cuba against any nation in the Western Hemisphere as an attack on the United States, requiring a full retaliatory response upon the Soviet Union."*

Finally, Khrushchev backed down. The crisis was over and the damaging aftermath of the Bay of Pigs apparently laid to rest.

Havana City,
Cuba

455 1963 ASSASSINATION OF JOHN F. KENNEDY

ON NOVEMBER 22, 1963, President Kennedy and his wife, Jacqueline, were conducting a tour of Dallas, Texas during an election trail. Shortly after noon, as the presidential motorcade passed the Texas School Depository, three gunshots rang out. Two bullets hit Kennedy in the head and neck, the third hit the Texan Governor, John Connally. The President was rushed to nearby Parkland Memorial Hospital, but at 1:00 PM he was pronounced dead.

A few hours later, a 24-year-old Texan named Lee Harvey Oswald was arrested for the assassination. Two days afterwards, as he was being transported from police headquarters to the county jail, Oswald was shot dead at point-blank range by strip-club owner, Jack Ruby.

As the nation mourned their president, conspiracy theories abounded. When Vice-President Lyndon B. Johnson was sworn in as President, he called for an enquiry, which after 10 months concluded that both Lee Harvey Oswald and Jack Ruby had acted entirely alone. This did little to quiet the conspiracy theorists. In 1976, the enquiry was re-launched by the House of Representatives Select Committee on Assassinations. It eventually concluded that Kennedy *"was probably assassinated as a result of a conspiracy."*

The assassination of President Kennedy remains the subject of widespread debate to this day.

456 1965-73 THE WAR IN VIETNAM

IN 1964, following an alleged attack on US destroyers in South Vietnam by North Vietnamese torpedo boats, the Gulf of Tonkin Resolution gave US President Lyndon permission to take *"all necessary measures to repel armed attack"* in Vietnam. Six months later, communist Viet Cong attacked a South Vietnamese US airbase and a brutal war was initiated. By the end of the year, at the request of the United States, South Korea, Australia, New Zealand, Thailand and the Philippines had entered the conflict.

Fighting was fierce, with the highly toxic defoliant, Agent Orange, being dropped across Vietnam, and US *"search and destroy"* missions killing civilians as well as the Viet Cong.

With over half a million American troops in Vietnam, a Tet Offensive, launched by the Viet Cong across South Vietnam in January 1968, swung American public opinion into the anti-war camp.

An American Tank destroyed by Viet Cong in Cu Chi

In March 1968, President Johnson called for renewed peace negotiations and a halt to bombing raids. But it was not until 1973, under President Nixon, that a peace agreement was reached. The agreement failed to solve the North-South Vietnam divide and in 1975 South Vietnam fell to the Communists. Having already lost 58,000 troops and spent over $100 billion during the war, the US failed to intervene.

457 1966–70 CULTURAL REVOLUTION IN CHINA

🎓 **DURING A MEETING** of the Central Committee in May 1966, Mao Zedung, Chairman of the Communist Party of China, announced his plans for a "new leap forward," or a "Cultural Revolution."

In the first "Great Leap Forward" in 1958, Mao had hoped to modernize China's economy by organizing the Chinese population into communes, in order to increase both agricultural and industrial production. The plan had backfired dramatically and led to food shortages, mass starvation, and severe economic regression.

458 FAST FACT...

📖 **IN 1970,** archaeologists excavating an ancient Egyptian tomb found the skeleton of a grave robber with his hand trapped in the coffin lid.

The Cultural Revolution was Mao's attempt to recover from this failure by reasserting his beliefs and authority, and by purging the nation of his rivals (those *"who have followed the path of capitalism"*) and the *"four olds"*: old ideas, culture, customs, and habits.

The Red Guards (organized groups of radical students) were given the task of eradicating the *"four olds."* Consequently, schools and colleges were closed and teachers, writers, scientists, engineers, and many figures of authority were criticized, persecuted, imprisoned or beaten to death. Mao removed all opponents from inside his own party. By the time the Revolution finally ended upon Mao's death in 1976, many relics and artefacts from China's historical and cultural past had been destroyed.

459 FAST FACT...

📖 **IN 1970,** an Arizona lawyer sued God for damages after a lightning bolt struck his secretary's home. God failed to appear in court.

460 1966 MARTIN LUTHER KING JR.

ONE OF THE MOST REVERED FIGURES of America's Civil Rights Movement, Martin Luther King Jr., was born in Atlanta, Georgia, on January 15, 1929, the son and grandson of local pastors. In 1954, Martin followed in their footsteps and became pastor of the Dexter Avenue Baptist Church in Montgomery, Alabama.

Already an active civil rights campaigner and member of the National Association for the Advancement of Colored People (NAACP), he came to the nation's attention when he successfully led the Montgomery Bus Boycott, the first non-violent demonstration of the Civil Rights Movement. In 1957, he was elected president of the Southern Christian Leadership Conference.

Motivated by the teachings and methods of India's Mahatma Gandhi, King advocated civil disobedience and non-violence. Over the next 10 years he traveled millions of miles, delivered countless speeches, and planned and led numerous civil rights marches.

In August 1963, King led 250,000 people in a peaceful march on Washington DC, where he delivered his world-famous "I have a dream" speech. In 1964 he was awarded the Nobel Peace Prize for his efforts to end racial discrimination.

On April 14, 1968, while standing on the balcony of a motel room in Memphis Tennessee, he was shot and killed by escaped convict, James Earl Ray. Like John F. Kennedy before him, King's assassination has attracted many conspiracy theories.

Martin Luther King, Jr Monument in Washington, DC

461 1967 THE SIX-DAY WAR

THE SIX-DAY WAR (or the Arab-Israeli War) took place on June 5–10, 1967. It was fought between Israel and its neighboring states of Jordan, Syria, and Egypt (the United Arab Republic).

Following the Suez Crisis of 1956, the United Nations had obtained the agreement of Middle Eastern nations to station peace-keeping forces along sensitive border lines. In 1967, Egypt requested the removal of these forces from the Suez region, deployed large forces in the Sinai Peninsula, and set up a naval blockade in the Gulf of Aqaba, which effectively cut off Israeli shipping routes. Israel viewed these actions as a direct threat to its territory.

In a pre-emptive move, Israel's Defence Minister, General Moshe Dayan, ordered a series of surprise air attacks, codenamed "Moked," on its supposed enemies.

The military campaign proved to be highly successful, with the Arab air forces targeted while still on the ground. Three hundred Egyptian aircraft and helicopters were destroyed in less than two hours. Jordan, Syrian, and Iraqi airfields were also targeted.

The decisive Israeli victory saw the nation gain control of the Gaza Strip, the Sinai Peninsula, the West Bank, East Jerusalem, and the Golan Heights.

Panorama of
Jerusalem, Israel

462 1969 THE MOON LANDING

RUSSIA'S SUCCESSFUL LAUNCH of the *Sputnik* satellite in 1957 had left America in shock. The launch of its successor, *Sputnik II*, only heightened America's sense of humiliation. Not only did Russian scientific and technological prowess outstrip that of America, but the success of *Sputnik* had also demonstrated that, unlike America, Russia had the capacity to launch intercontinental ballistic missiles.

463 FAST FACT...

📖 **THE 1974** *The Guinness Book of Records* earned a place in its own pages by becoming the world's fastest-selling book.

During Kennedy's administration, the space race had become a military exercise, with Kennedy persuading Congress to prioritize work at the National Aeronautics and Space Administration (NASA). Congress approved a billion-dollar investment in the space program and in May 1961, America sent its first astronaut into space.

When Nixon came to office in 1969, he continued to support the space program with the ultimate goal of a manned moon landing. Finally, on July 20, 1969, the world watched in wonder as Neil Armstrong stepped out of the lunar module, *Eagle*, and onto the surface of the moon, uttering the now-famous words, *"That was one small step for man, one giant leap for mankind."*

464 1972–74 THE WATERGATE SCANDAL

ON JUNE 17, 1972, during the United States presidential elections, a security guard at the Watergate apartment complex in Washington DC alerted the police to a break-in at the offices of the Democrat Party headquarters. Police arrested five men at the scene, all of whom were carrying papers indicating that they were employed by the Committee to Re-elect the President (CREEP). The burglary was reported in the press, but nothing connected the men to the White House. Consequently the incident had no impact on the elections and Richard Nixon won by a landslide.

465 FAST FACT...

FOR JAPANESE SOLDIER
Shoichi Yokoi, World War II ended in 1972 when he emerged from Guam Island, where he had been hiding out for 28 years.

Questions began to be asked when it emerged that the men arrested were a former FBI agent, a former CIA agent, and three Cubans, who had each been involved in the Bay of Pigs fiasco.

466 FAST FACT...

"There can be no whitewash at the White House." – US President Richard Nixon, May 1973, speaking of the Watergate Scandal.

Rumors of high-level corruption began to circulate after two investigative journalists from the *Washington Post* published a series of stories. They claimed that the burglary had been carried out on White House orders, and that White House officials had subsequently made attempts to bury the evidence. The Senate responded by appointing a Select Committee to launch an investigation into the Watergate scandals. Their findings culminated in Nixon being charged with a list of *"high crimes and misdemeanours,"* and resulted in his resignation on August 8, 1974.

467 FAST FACT...

THE FIRST EMAIL was sent in 1971 by Ray Tomlinson, an employee at a technology research company.

468 1976 THE KHMER ROUGE GENOCIDE

ESTABLISHED IN 1960 by Cambodian revolutionary Pol Pot, the Kampuchean People's Party (or the Khmer Rouge) was a radical communist movement dedicated to ridding Cambodia of Western influences, and instating a purely agrarian society, or peasant economy.

In 1970, with the backing of North Vietnamese and Viet Cong troops, the Khmer Rouge instigated a civil war that was to last until April 17, 1975, when they captured the capital city of Phnom Penh and installed a new government (the Kampuchean People's Republic).

The new regime and Pol Pot's vision of "Year Zero" was immediately put into effect. Entire cities were evacuated and the citizens forced to march out to the countryside, where they were organized into vast collective farms. The old and infirm were left on roadsides to die, children were separated from parents, and anyone deemed lazy was eliminated. Schools, hospitals, and factories were closed, the currency was abolished, and the interrogation center, S-21, was established, where more than 500,000 Cambodians were executed. Under one of the twentieth century's most violent regimes, an estimated two million Cambodians died.

When the city of Phnom Penh was captured by Vietnamese troops in January 1979, Pol Pot escaped by helicopter and the Khmer Rouge was forced into the jungle.

469 FAST FACT...

IN 1972, a plane crashed in the Andes. Rescuers arrived 70 days later. Those still living had survived by eating the passengers who had died.

470 FAST FACT...

"I don't think there will be a woman prime minister in my lifetime." – Margaret Thatcher, 5 March 1973

471 FAST FACT...

US INVENTOR Art Fry hated the way slips of paper he used as bookmarks kept falling out. In 1974 he came up with the Post-it note.

IN 1978, after years of popular opposition to its policies and following several coups, the Afghan monarchy, under Sardar Khan, was overthrown and a pro-Soviet Communist government under Noor Taraki was put in place. In 1979, when another coup saw Taraki ousted and Hafizullah Amin installed as president, the Soviet government decided to intervene. Soviet troops were sent into Afghanistan, Amin was executed, and a Soviet-backed president, Babrak Karmal, was installed.

The Soviet invasion was opposed by Afghan guerrilla forces known as *mujahidin* (Islamic warriors). Although greatly outnumbered by Soviet forces, the mujahidin received backing from the US, China, Saudi Arabia, and Iran and were able to hold out against Soviet and government forces until a stalemate was reached. The war dragged on for 10 years, claiming the lives of over one million Afghans and 15,000 Soviet soldiers. The country and its economy were devastated.

In 1989, the Soviet Union withdrew its troops and the guerrilla forces began to move in on the government, eventually capturing the capital, Kabul, in 1992. But in-fighting amongst different factions of the guerrillas resulted in a divided Afghanistan. By 1994, a new faction of Islamic fundamentalists, known as the Taliban, had emerged as a growing power.

Kabul, Afghanistan

473 1979 JOHN PAUL II BECOMES POPE

BORN IN WADOWICE, Poland, in 1920, Karol Wojtyla lost his mother, father, and brother at an early age. He enrolled at the Jagiellonian University in Krakow when he was 19 and shortly afterwards began to study for the priesthood.

474 FAST FACT...

IN 1977, a US forest ranger, Roy Sullivan, set a world record when he was struck by lightning for the seventh time – and survived.

Karol was ordained on November 1, 1946 and began working with Polish refugees in France, before returning to Poland to teach ethics at the Catholic University of Lublin. In 1964, he was appointed Archbishop of Krakow and on May 29, 1967, he was made Cardinal by Pope Paul VI.

Karol proved himself a formidable supporter of the Church's right to free expression of opinion. He was a fervent anti-communist and possessed a sharp intellect.

Following the death of Pope Paul VI in August 1978, and the sudden death of his successor (Pope John Paul I) only one month into his pontificate, the cardinals assembled in Rome and elected Karol Wojtyla to be the first non-Italian pope in 455 years, and the first ever Slavic pope.

475 FAST FACT...

IN 1978, after a 10-year-effort, the disease smallpox was eradicated – the first disease to be wiped out by human efforts.

Named Pope John Paul II in honor of his predecessor, he is remembered for his tolerant and charismatic nature and his contribution towards the peaceful dissolution of the Soviet Union in 1991.

476 FAST FACT...

THE FINAL VICTIM of the guillotine, Hamida Djandoubi, was beheaded in Marseilles, France, on September 10, 1977.

477 1980 MUGABE WINS POWER IN SOUTHERN RHODESIA

🎓 **BORN THE SON OF A CARPENTER** on February 21, 1924 in Kutama, Southern Rhodesia, Robert Mugabe trained to be a teacher and was first introduced to nationalist politics while a student. He played a major role in the formation of the Zimbabwe African National Union (ZANU) and in 1964 was imprisoned for 10 years, accused of "subversive speech." While still in prison, Mugabe was elected leader of ZANU, taking over from Ndabaningi Sithole.

On his release from prison in 1975, Mugabe was jointly instrumental – along with Joshua Nkomo – in leading the Patriotic Front of Zimbabwe (PF) against the white-ruled Rhodesian government during the civil war of 1975–79. When the war ended, Mugabe's newly named ZANU-PF party won the 1980 parliamentary elections following negotiations held in London, and he was voted prime minister.

Mugabe formed a coalition government with Nkomo's ZAPU (Zimbabwe African People's Union) party, but ousted Nkomo from power in 1982. Two years later, the parties merged again to form the ZANU-Patriotic Front in an attempt by Mugabe to transform the parliamentary democracy into a one-party socialist state.

Mugabe has served as President of Zimbabwe since 1987. His rule has been marked by much political turmoil, accusations of violence and intimidation, and foreign criticism of his policies, which have led to the deterioration of the Zimbabwean economy.

478 1982 FALKLANDS WAR

🎓 **THE FALKLAND ISLANDS** are situated some 400 miles off the South American mainland and in 1982 had a population of 1820.

The islands had been claimed by Argentina after it had won independence from Spain in 1816. But in 1833, as the Napoleonic Wars ended, Argentinean settlers were evicted from the islands by a British Naval expedition, and the Falklands were declared part of the British Empire.

Argentina had never accepted the British claim, and it was this long-standing dispute over the sovereignty of the islands that led to an Argentinean invasion on April 2, 1982.

479 FAST FACT...

📖 **THE FIRST PERSON** to receive an artificial heart was Barney Clark in 1982. The aluminum and plastic device kept him alive for 112 more days.

It seemed a pointless conflict from the very beginning. The islands had been occupied by the British since 1833, the inhabitants wished to remain British, and under the UN charter small nations had the right to National Self Determination.

As Argentinean troops landed on the islands, the British government severed all diplomatic ties with Argentina and readied its navy for action. When Argentina ignored the UN Security Council's Resolution 502 calling for peaceful negotiations, the British moved its task force into Falkland waters.

The war was marked by the sinking of a number of British and Argentinean ships, including the Argentine vessel, the *General Belgrano*. The Argentineans surrendered 74 days later on June 14, 1982.

King penguins march along the beach at Volunteer Point in the Falkland Islands

480 1989 BERLIN WALL TORN DOWN

🎓 **IN THE LATE 1980'S,** the communist grip on the Eastern Bloc began to weaken. In 1987, in a speech made at the Brandenburg Gate to commemorate the 750th anniversary of Berlin, US President Ronald Reagan challenged the General Secretary of the Soviet Union Communist Party, Mikhail Gorbachev, to *"tear down this wall."*

At midnight on November 9, 1989, East German government official, Gunther Schabowski, announced that, *"Permanent relocations can be done through all border checkpoints between the GDR into the FRG or West Berlin."* After nearly 30 years of containment, jubilant East Berliners began to pour through the Wall. It was soon after demolished and the stage was set for the reunification of East and West Germany into a single German state on October 3, 1990.

481 1989 TIANANMEN SQUARE

🎓 **CHINA HAD ALREADY** lived through the terror and hardships of Mao Zedung's "Great Leap Forward" and the Cultural Revolution of 1966–76, which saw millions of Chinese citizens die through starvation, torture or murder, and much of China's traditional culture and religions destroyed.

As the Chinese people looked to the reforms being made in the communist countries of East Europe, grievances towards their own government deepened. When government reformist Hu Yaobang (General Secretary of the Communist Party of China) was forced out of office and publicly humiliated for his ideas, public anger was roused. When Yaobang died on April 15, 1989, student protestors called for him to be pardoned and given a State funeral. To their surprise, the government consented and the encouraged students began to gather on the streets of Beijing to call for social, economic, and political reforms.

The protests grew into a mass movement and on May 20, 1989, a disquieted Chinese government declared martial law. On June 4, 1989, as protestors gathered in Tiananmen Square, the People's Liberation Army marched in and opened fire, killing an estimated 2–7,000 people. The Tiananmen Square protests halted any reforms and China closed itself to international criticism.

482 1991 THE WORLD WIDE WEB

BRITISH COMPUTER SCIENTIST, Sir Tim Berners-Lee, was born in London on June 8, 1955. He graduated from Queens College Oxford in 1976, with a degree in physics. In 1980, while working as a contractor for CERN (the European Particle Physics laboratory in Geneva, Switzerland) he first proposed the idea of exchanging information among researchers using the concept of hypertext (that is, text displayed on a computer with references to other text, which can be accessed by clicking a computer mouse or by a key-press sequence). With this in mind, he developed a simple hypertext program named ENQUIRE.

When Berners-Lee returned to CERN in 1989, it had the largest Internet node in Europe and he instantly saw the benefits in joining his hypertext idea with the Internet, announcing that he intended to use hypertext, *"to link and access information of various kinds as a web of nodes in which the user can browse at will."*

The global hypertext project, begun in October 1990 and known as the World Wide Web, saw Berners-Lee write the first WWW server, *"httpd."*

By 1991, browser, web pages and web server software were ready, and on August 6, 1991, the World Wide Web became available to the public.

---

483 FAST FACT...

DURING the Liberian civil war (1989–1996), General Joshua Milton Blahyl was famous for leading his army into battle naked, except for his boots and gun.

484 FAST FACT...

THE WORLD'S FIRST ice hotel was built in Sweden in 1990. It has 80 rooms, a bar and reception. It melts every April and must be rebuilt each winter.

485 1994 NELSON MANDELA VOTED PRESIDENT

BORN THE SON of the Chief of the Tembu Tribe in Transkei, South Africa, on July 18, 1918, Nelson Mandela attended the University of Witwatersrand and earned a degree in law at the age of 24.

In 1944 he joined the African National Congress (ANC), and when the pro-apartheid National Party came to power in 1948, he became actively involved in protesting against their racial segregation policies.

486 FAST FACT...

IN 1995, 26-year-old banker Nick Leeson single-handedly brought down Barings, Britain's oldest bank. His secret trading deals caused losses of £827 million.

487 FAST FACT...

THE FIRST ever space funeral took place on February 9, 1997. The ashes of several famous Americans were placed aboard a rocket and fired into space.

Initially influenced by India's Mahatma Gandhi, Mandela advocated non-violent protest methods until he was arrested on December 5, 1956, and charged with treason. Acquitted in 1961, Mandela co-founded an armed wing of the ANC known as Umkhonto we Sizwe (Spear of the Nation), and organized sabotage campaigns against the military and the government. In 1962, Mandela was arrested and sentenced to five years in prison. While incarcerated, he was brought to stand trial alongside other members of the ANC accused of capital crimes of sabotage. Mandela received a life sentence.

His years in prison saw his reputation as an important black leader soar, and when he was released from prison on February 11, 1990, he was elected President of the ANC. Four years later during South Africa's first multi-racial elections on April 27, 1994, Mandela won 62% of the vote and became South Africa's first black President.

488 FAST FACT...

IN 1996, McDonalds opened the its first *"ski-thru"* restaurant in Sweden.

489 FAST FACT...

NOVEMBER 1997 saw the first ever space vote. Astronaut David Wolf, aboard the *Mir* space station, emailed his vote for mayor of Houston.

☞ ON SEPTEMBER 11, 2001,
the world was shocked and horrified to witness a series of terrorist attacks on landmark buildings in the United States. Nineteen men with links to the Islamic terrorist group, al-Qaeda, simultaneously hijacked four passenger aircraft (American Airlines Flight 11, United Airlines Flight 175, American Airlines Flight 77, and United Airlines Flight 93) with the express intention of crashing them into major buildings.

At 8:46 AM, five of the men crashed American Airlines Flight 11 into the North Tower of the World Trade Centre. A few minutes later at 9:03 AM, five more of the hijackers crashed United Airlines Flight 17 into the Trade Centre's South Tower. At 9:37 AM, American Airlines Flight 77 was crashed into the Pentagon in Arlington, Virginia. The fourth plane, United Airlines Flight 93, crashed in a field near Shanksville, Pennsylvania, after passengers attempted to wrest control of it from the hijackers. It is thought the hijackers' intended target was the White House or the United States Capitol.

491 FAST FACT...

📖 **THE LONGEST-LIVING** person in history was Jeanne Calment of France, who died in 1997, aged 122.

492 FAST FACT...

📖 *"They misunderestimated me."* – US President George W. Bush

493 FAST FACT...

📖 **IN MAY 2000**, Filipino students released the *ILOVEYOU* email virus. It quickly spread, infecting millions of PCs and causing over US$10 billion in damage.

494 FAST FACT...

📖 **IN 2003** the human genome project was completed. It revealed we only have twice as many genes as a fruit fly, and share 60% of our genes with the banana.

Nearly 3000 people from 57 different countries were killed in the attacks. It became the most media-covered event of all time and had a profound effect on the entire world. The US has since launched a campaign to combat terrorism.

496 2008 OBAMA ELECTED US PRESIDENT

BARACK OBAMA was born in Honolulu, Hawaii on August 4, 1961. His father and mother were both students at the University of Hawaii. They divorced when Obama was two and he was brought up in Hawaii by his mother and grandparents.

Obama graduated from Columbia University in New York and went on to work as a community advisor in Chicago. In 1988, he attended Harvard Law School and became the first African-American president of the Harvard Law Review. After graduating in 1991 with a J.D. magna cum laude, he published a book, *Dreams of my Father*, and taught law at the University of Chicago Law School.

In 1997, Obama was elected to the Illinois State Senate and served as chairman of the Public health and Welfare Committee. In July 2004 he delivered the keynote address at the Democratic National Convention and in the November 2004 general election he was voted the fifth African-American US Senator in history, winning 70% of the vote.

On February 10, 2007, Obama announced his entry into the US Presidential race. He beat his Democratic rival, Hilary Clinton, and on January 2, 2009, went on to beat the Republican candidate, Senator John McCain, to become the United State's 44th – and the first African-American – president.

495 FAST FACT...

📖 *"The largest financial crisis of its kind in human history."* – Bank of England Deputy Governor Charlie Bean, describing the 2008–9 banking collapse.

497 FAST FACT...

📖 *"People have called me 'Alabama' or 'Yo Mama'"* – Barack Obama, speaking about his unusual name.

498 2010 THE ARAB SPRING

ON DECEMBER 16, 2010, an unemployed Tunisian college graduate, Mohammed Bouazizi, was selling fruit and vegetables in the town of Sidi Bouzid without a permit. He was confronted by a policewoman who spat in his face and confiscated his cart. The following day, Bouazizi set himself alight, and in the process ignited a wave of demonstrations and protests across the Arab states, which has come to be known as the Arab Spring.

499 FAST FACT...

ON CHRISTMAS DAY 2009, a terrorist on board a flight from Amsterdam to Detroit attempted to detonate explosives hidden in his underwear.

Starting in Tunisia, public anger over poverty, injustice, unemployment, corruption, and human rights violations, exploded into violent confrontations with the security forces, which led to the ousting of Tunisian President Ben Ali on January 14, 2011.

The protests quickly spread through the Arab world, and on February 11, 2011, Egypt's leader, Hosni Mubarak, was also forced to step down, but not before hundreds of protestors had been killed by Egyptian security forces.

As Egyptians celebrated in Cairo's Thrir Square, violent protests in Libya turned to civil war, leading to the killing of Libyan leader Muammar Gaddafi and the overthrowing of the government.

To date, uprisings in Yemini, Syria, Kuwait, Lebanon, Oman, and Morocco have stimulated government reforms, while other countries such as Iraq and Algeria are experiencing ongoing dissent.

500 FAST FACT...

THE FIRST all-robotic surgery was performed at a Montreal hospital on October 13, 2010. The robot anesthetist was called McSleepy.

501 FAST FACT...

"We got him." – US President Barack Obama on hearing of the death of terrorist Osama bin Laden, killed in a CIA operation on May 2, 2011.

INDEX